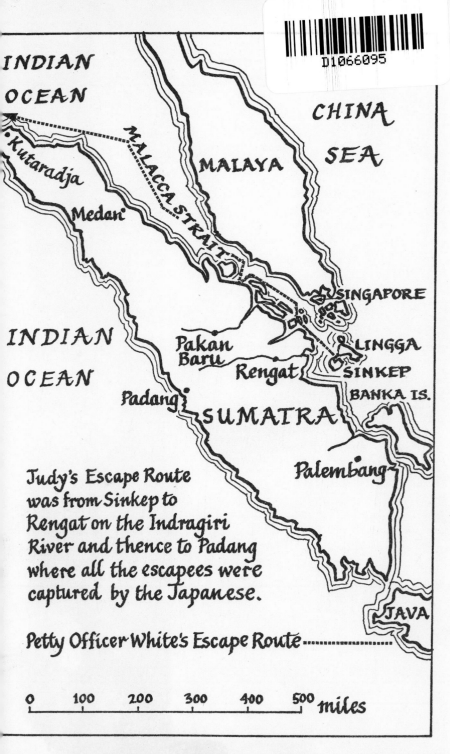

INDIAN
OCEAN

CHINA

SEA

Kutaradja

MALAYA

MALACCA STRAIT

Medan

SINGAPORE

INDIAN

OCEAN

Pakan
Baru

Rengat

LINGGA

SINKEP

BANKA IS.

Padang

SUMATRA

Palembang

Judy's Escape Route
was from Sinkep to
Rengat on the Indragiri
River and thence to Padang
where all the escapees were
captured by the Japanese.

Petty Officer White's Escape Route ·····················

JAVA

0      100      200      300      400      500  miles

THE JUDY STORY
*THE DOG WITH SIX LIVES*

# THE JUDY STORY
## THE DOG WITH SIX LIVES

E. VARLEY

Edited by Wendy James

SOUVENIR PRESS

First published 1973 by Souvenir Press Ltd.
95 Mortimer Street, London W.1 and
simultaneously in Canada by J. M. Dent & Sons
(Canada) Ltd., Ontario, Canada

Reprinted November 1973

ISBN 0 285 62121 1

Printed in Great Britain by
Bristol Typesetting Co., Ltd.
Bristol

## Dedication

This story is dedicated to those of our comrades who, after much hardship and suffering, did not return to their Homeland. And it is also dedicated to animal lovers throughout the world.

## Acknowledgements

WE WISH TO THANK

The Rt. Hon. The Earl of Avon, K.C., P.C., M.C.
Lt. Cdr. C.R. H. Broadway, R.N.
Naval Historical Branch, M.O.D., London.
The Australian Naval Representative, London.
The President, Officers and Members of the R.N.A., Portsmouth.
V. Rigby, Imperial War Museum, London.
A. Toussaint, Chief Archivist, Port Louis, Mauritius.
The Secretary, The Institute of Marine Engineers, London.
The Area Commissioner, Ministry of Regional and Rural Development, Nachingwea, Tanzania.
Arthur Dean, Taikoo, B & S.
Captain D. C. Sims, Merchant Navy.
Captain Donald Brotchie, Merchant Navy.
Mrs. K. Edmonton, Secretary to the Pointer Club of Great Britain.
Mr. and Mrs. Bill Shakespeare.
Geoffrey H. Gompertz.
Hilton Stainton, Australia.
Frank Sawyer, Australia.
Commodore G. R. Villar, D.S.O., R.N.
Captain G. M. K. Brewer, R.N.
Lt. R. L. Smith, R.A.N.

Col. R. H. Senior (rtd.), Royal Artillery Records.
The Keeper, The Public Service Records, London.
The Chief Hydrographer to the Government of India.
Vosper Thorneycroft Group, Portsmouth.
John Stretton, *The News*, Portsmouth.
John Swires & Sons Ltd., London.
Jardine Matheson & Co. Ltd., Hong Kong.
Mr. and Mrs. L. Perry, Farnham.
C. Agerter, P.D.S.A.
W. H. Betenon, Fareham, Hants.

Special thanks to those men and women whose anecdotes have brought to life the story of Judy, and to Frank Williams who was so helpful and informative during his visit to this country in March, 1972.

# Contents

# Foreword

by Rear Admiral F. B. P. Brayne-Nicholls CB, DSC

THE DOG, man's faithful friend, stands first and foremost among the many animals made use of by man.

Ever since the days of the Stone Age, the dog has taken part in man's activities both in peace and war, and it naturally followed that, from time to time, the heroism and sacrifices of one particular dog would stand out above all others.

Now we have, at last, the full story of Judy, the pedigree pointer bitch who waged her own particular war against the Japanese.

The late Mrs. Maria E. Dickin, founder of the People's Dispensary for Sick Animals, also founded an award for animals which had been recommended by military authorities for special war service—The Dickin Medal, sometimes known as the Animal VC.

It gave her particular pleasure, I am sure, to authorise the award of the Dickin Medal to Judy with a citation that read :—

"For magnificent courage and endurance in Japanese prison camps which helped to maintain morale among her fellow prisoners, and also for saving many lives through her intelligence and watchfulness."

This is an amazing story—but then, Judy was an amazing dog.

## Introduction

HMS *Excellent*, the Royal Navy's Gunnery School on Whale Island in Portsmouth Harbour, is recognised and accepted as "The World's Gunnery School".

From here, between the wars, the Royal Navy's Gunnery Ratings marched forth to join the ships of the greatest Navy the world has ever seen—or will ever see again.

Great ships with names that were household words— *Hood, Repulse, Nelson, Rodney, Eagle, Tiger.*

Ships that reached the world's headlines in a blaze of glory—*Cossack, Exeter, Ark Royal, Kelly, Glowworm, Glorious, Amethyst.*

Ships that were unheard of, unsung—like the Yangtse River Gunboats, small ships doing big jobs in comparative obscurity.

It was to praise these little ships that a group of men got together on a cold night in February 1970 for the first annual reunion of the Yangtse Gunboatmen's Association.

Cigars smouldered; the beer flowed; the volume of conversation increased. The Admirals, looking down from their huge gilt frames appeared to nod their heads in silent approval as the men of the Gunboats recaptured and relived their years on the mighty Yangtse River—dangerous, exciting, action-packed years.

And in a special place of honour on the wall was a painting, life-size, showing the head and shoulders of a dog, a liver-and-white pointer, framed in a ship's cowl.

Judy of Sussex, Judy RN, Judy POW—no reunion would be complete without her.

At that reunion she was talked about so much that immediately after, four ex-Gunboatmen who had, in different ways, shared the dangers and excitements of both Gunboat and POW life with Judy, decided to put together the full story of her life.

They searched official records, wrote letters by the score, visited places, interviewed people. They travelled far and wide in their search for missing links.

The four men were : Ex-Chief Petty Officer Vic Oliver (HMS *Gnat*); Ex-Chief SBA Bill Wilson (HMS *Gnat*); Ex-Petty Officer Coxswain George White (HMS *Grasshopper*); Ex-Petty Officer Stoker Les Searle (HMS *Dragonfly*).

This is their story of a dog who was a legend in her own lifetime, a dog who is remembered by people all around the world.

# I  *Judy Joins the Navy*

SHE HAD no name—in fact, she had very little of anything. She had big brown eyes—appealing eyes that said, " I'll lick your boots if you don't kick me." She had a moist, pointed nose, a tail that would have wagged at the least sign of encouragement, and a liver-and-white body that would have been quite cuddly if the ribs had not been so conspicuous.

She had no home. For some months she had lived, survived, in an old cardboard box behind the shop run by the Chinese man Soo. It was not the most comfortable of homes, but it did, at least, shield her from the cold night winds.

There was much to worry about in this Shanghai of 1936 but somehow the kindly Soo managed to find scraps of food which he dropped into the box.

Then one even more miserable day sailors from a visiting Japanese Gunboat got into a fight with Soo. Strong words were followed by stronger blows until Soo's pathetic little shop lay in ruins.

The pup, whimpering with anxiety and concern, crawled out of her box, flat on her belly, only to meet a wildly-aimed kick which sent her sprawling across the narrow street into a pile of rubbish.

Huddled there she did not whimper again. She was not yet six months old but she was fast learning the essentials of survival. She stayed in a shop doorway for a long time,

and even though the sailors were gone she could go no
further. Her pads were sore, she was cold, and she was very,
very hungry.

She was crying silently to herself but the only sign of her
suffering was an occasional spasmodic jerk of her small
body such as can be seen when a child sobs.

"Shudi! Oh, Shudi! Where you been?"

So miserable was she that her tail hardly moved, although
recognition was mutual. Suddenly she was lifted into the
cradling arms of Lee Ming, the little Chinese girl whose
mother worked, and lived, at the Shanghai Dog Kennels.

The little girl had immediately recognised the pup as
being the one which, some months before, had wriggled
under the fencing surrounding the kennels. No one could
stop her and she disappeared into the overcrowded streets
of Shanghai.

With the pup, already fast asleep cuddled in the warm
depths of her jacket, Lee Ming ran to the large house in
the Kennels Compound and rushed into the Reception
Room where an English woman sat at a big desk.

Lee Ming opened her jacket.

"Look, I find Shudi," she said, panting for breath.

The woman stood up, leaned over the desk and took
the pup from the little girl's arms. She stroked the small
body, fondled its ears. The pup opened one eye, showed a
pink tongue, went back to sleep.

The woman looked at the girl, and smiled. "It really is
the one that ran away. I think we should give her a bath
and a good dinner, don't you?"

The girl nodded eagerly, held out welcoming arms to
the pup.

"Lee Ming," said the woman, "why do you call her
Shudi?" Lee Ming turned towards her, then looked down
at the pup, again cradled in her jacket. "I always call this
one Shudi. Shudi means peaceful—and that is how she
looks, doesn't she?"

The woman touched the girl's head and said: "Yes,

Lee Ming, she does, and that shall be her name—Judy."

*     *     *

Shanghai, in the autumn of 1936, was already feeling
the stirrings of the wind of change—a fearful, dreadful
wind that would, within months, scream like a raging fury
through the big cities and Treaty Ports of China, bringing
death and destruction, bullets and bayonets, pillage and
rape, to horrify the onlooking—but non-interfering—
world.

Imperial Japan was flexing her muscles and, even then,
planning the eventual domination of the Eastern World.
The occupation of Chinese ports would be the first of
many blows aimed at the two World Powers which were
regarded by Japan as her main enemies—Great Britain and
America.

While all this was being planned there were men—and
it is fortunate for Great Britain and for the rest of the
world that there have always been such men—who were
kept busy with the job in hand.

The men were the crews of the Royal Navy's River
Gunboats, and their job was to patrol more than a thousand miles of the mighty Yangtse River, to protect
shipping, repel pirates and to discourage bandits.

The lower reaches of the river, a distance of roughly six
hundred miles—were patrolled by Gunboats of the "Insect"
Class. One of these, HMS *Gnat*, had been in for her
annual refit and was preparing to leave the dock at
Shanghai to return to patrol duties.

Of less than 650 tons displacement, she was small enough
to navigate the many tricky parts of the river, with its
sandbanks and fast currents, yet big enough to carry quite
an imposing armament of two six-inch guns, one Vickers,
an anti-aircraft gun and machine-guns. Flat-bottomed,
drawing only a few feet of water as her twin screws revolved
in specially designed tunnels, her triple rudders and speed

of fourteen knots enabled her to easily manoeuvre against the strongest currents.

On a September afternoon the last of the stores and ammunition had been stowed away. The final touches of wet paint had been applied. The Chinese mess-boys had returned on board and were preparing afternoon tea on the messdeck.

Some of the seamen were already on the messdeck, preparing to change into clean white uniforms for their last evening ashore, when the head of the Coxswain appeared, upside down, through the open hatch, like an inverted pantomime demon. The mouth opened.

"All hands on deck in ten minutes."

The head disappeared.

"Now what," said one Able Seaman as he thrust one leg into a pair of freshly-ironed white trousers, "can be up?"

"It's about the new ship's pet," answered a voice from the other end of the messdeck.

The crew of the *Gnat* were grouped on the upper deck and the Coxswain called them to attention before reporting.

"Ship's Company mustered, Sir."

The First Lieutenant stepped up on to the ammunition case that had been hastily brought forward as a makeshift dais; gave the order "Stand Easy" before addressing the assembled men.

"A few weeks ago," he began, "the canteen committee, with myself as chairman, passed a resolution to the effect that we would have a ship's pet."

He looked down at the pieces of paper in his hand before continuing.

"I have studied your very interesting suggestions, most of which regretfully I had to discard as being impracticable, and then decided that our ship's pet should have three qualifications. Because we can do with some feminine companionship, the first qualification was—to be female. Secondly, she would be attractive, and thirdly she would have to earn her keep."

"On the *Bee* they have two cats. The *Cricket* has a dog —of sorts. The *Cicala* has a monkey, heaven help them. From this point on future shooting parties from this ship will no longer be able to return aboard with one duckling while stoutly averring that they shot down twenty-three."

He turned his head; called out: "Quartermaster!"

The Quartermaster appeared from the superstructure doorway. Beside him, on a lead and looking a little apprehensive, trotted Judy. They halted in the open space between the officer and the men. Judy sat down; her tongue lolled out as she appeared to give everyone a big grin.

"Here she is, then, gentlemen," said the First Lieutenant. "Meet the first lady of the Gunboats. Meet Judy— RN."

And so Judy joined the Navy and became for the next six years the only static member of the Gunboat Flotilla.

Chief Petty Officer Charles Jeffery was the Chief Bosun's mate on *Gnat* from 1936-8. He was known as the Chief Buffer, the man in the middle between the ship's company and the officers. In his diary he recorded:

"Judy of Sussex is a thoroughbred pointer coloured brown and white. She is a most lovable creature. As the Captain and I had been the ones to buy her for the ship's company he decided I should try to keep her forward so that she would not get too familiar with the men and so spoil our chances to train her for the gun. We soon found this was impossible. The ship's company treat and love Judy as a pet and I am delighted that the men share her. But of course our chances of making her a trained gun dog are very small."

The officers' messboy agreed with this. In fact, he boldly asserted that Judy only went rigid (as good pointers do when detecting game) when she could smell dinner, and that she could only "point" in one direction—towards the ship's galley!

She was given an official ship's book number, an open-topped box and a ship's blanket were provided as her sleeping quarters. It was agreed that only one man should be responsible for seeing to her strictly regulated meals, and that she should not be offered tit-bits at meal times. Definitely out were bars of chocolate and glasses of beer. (China gunboats were unique. They carried beer stocks on board and every crew member received a daily allowance.)

"Tankey"—otherwise Able Seaman Jan Cooper—was the natural and obvious choice for the new post of "Keeper of the Ship's Dog". As well as being in charge of all stores and fresh water, Able Seaman Cooper was also the ship's butcher, a job which, as Judy doubtless realised, offered many advantages.

Judy explored every nook and cranny of her new home. She knew which areas were forbidden to her, except by special invitation, and she knew she was not very welcome in the domains of the Chinese mess-boys and cooks. In fact, as C.P.O. Jeffery wrote in his diary : "She just tolerates the Chinese crewmen on board."

It was in November, however, that she came very close to losing her life for the second time.

C.P.O. Jeffery was coming aft when he saw that Judy had crawled through the port side guard rails on to the slippery steel plates outboard. He saw her fall over the side into the murky river and he shouted to the Captain, Lieutenant Commander the Hon. J. Waldegrave, that Judy was overboard. "Stop and full astern," he yelled, for the current was so strong he knew that Judy would be lost if the action weren't immediate. "The Captain knew what was required and he did just that," wrote C.P.O. Jeffery in his diary.

The Leading Stoker had also seen Judy go overboard and the power-boat was quickly manned and ready to be lowered when the ship stopped. Even in that short time Judy was no more than a small black dot rapidly disappearing in the fast-running river.

Leading Seaman Vic Oliver was coxswain of the boat and had with him an engine man and a Chinese boat boy named Wugle. As the current was about ten knots and the water was choppy and muddy, the boat went past Judy and turned back. Wugle leaned over the side to grab the dog's collar and both were in the water!

Round went the boat again and this time Wugle and Judy were both dragged aboard. Their recovery was greeted with cheers for many men had lost their lives in the treacherous Yangtse—not only was there no buoyancy but the currents were notoriously strong.

The boat headed back to the ship and with the tiller gripped firmly between his thighs, leading seaman Oliver sent a brief signal in semaphore "Christening completed".

Willings hands helped them aboard and Wugle disappeared below to wash off the mud.

The doctor ordered that the bedraggled dog be washed in disinfectant and C.P.O. Jeffery "bathed her in a hip bath and dried her with my towels.

"She was a bit scared at first and shaky, but I talked to her and walked her round the ship. She slept next to my bunk that night and next day was quite O.K."

Even though she wasn't a man, the incident was recorded in the ship's log as : Exercised Man Overboard and Away Lifeboat's Crew.

Judy had learnt her lesson. From then on she gave the ship's guard rails a wide berth. Even when "navigating" the gangway from ship to shore, she was on the alert with, as Leading Seaman Oliver observed, "Ears at the cocked position, and all systems at ready."

## 2 *The Talents Begin to Show*

HMS GNAT, back on patrol duty, ploughed her nose into the swiftly-running waters of the Yangtse River. But for the two funnels standing side by side on the squat super-structure just behind the bridge, the Gunboat looked very much like an elongated Liverpool tram.

The *Gnat*—as did all other shipping on the river—steamed by day, but anchored at night. There was, there-fore, no day and night watchkeeping, each day being one of normal duties and routines for the thirty-eight mem-bers of the Ship's company. At night, the Duty Quarter-master would take on the additional duties of guard and lookout.

Now, two days out from Shanghai after the refit, the guns had been tested; the gun crews had been exercised. The searchlight had been switched on and off. The Aldis lamp had blinked long messages at no one in particular. Ammunition lockers and magazines had been finally squared off.

Tankey, with Judy in close attendance, inspected the supplementary food stocks—a number of live chickens which would be kept in large wicker baskets on the upper deck until they were needed.

This done, he decided to try and teach Judy how to "point". He had explained, with the utmost patience, what would be required of her. He even tried to show her, in stiff-armed mimicry, just how it should be done.

Judy watched his strange antics with some concern, her head quizzically to one side. She was not getting the message. Every day he repeated the exercise, hoping that the miracle would occur, that she would understand. But she didn't and after a while he began to think she was enjoying the whole thing—he was her own special entertainment!

Despite this she proved her worth in a spectacular way —by developing an early warning system to warn of the approach of the open cess boats which were a constant hazard of the river.

Judy's rude barking, rising to a crescendo, proved invaluable for it gave the men time to batten down all hatches and portholes against the overpowering and sickening stench.

At Wuhu the *Gnat* tied up alongside another Gunboat of the Insect Class, the *Ladybird*, whereupon officers and men were invited aboard each other's ship where rum tots were shared and friendships renewed.

One member of the *Ladybird*'s ship's company, however, was *not* welcomed aboard the *Gnat*—their ship's pet, Bonzo.

Bonzo was a dog, a large well-built dog. Half boxer, half terrier, it was soon apparent that he had taken a strong fancy to Judy so Tankey made sure that Judy was kept securely under lock and key until the other Gunboat, with the disappointed Bonzo on board, departed on her way down river.

The *Gnat* continued on her way and it was just above Wuhu where the river narrowed appreciably that Judy showed first signs of an uncanny talent.

The *Gnat* was anchored for the night, and just after three o'clock in the morning, Judy jumped out from her box on the bridge. Obviously wildly excited she began to bark, her fury apparently concentrated on something or someone ahead of the *Gnat*.

The sentry didn't hesitate—he switched on the Aldis lamp and beamed it ahead of *Gnat*'s bows. As the beam swept over the two big junks drifting down towards him, he drew and fired his pistol—the urgent and unmistakable danger signal which brought the pyjama-clad crew of the *Gnat* to their predetermined stations, rifles or pistols at the ready.

The sentry, ordering Judy to be quiet realised that river pirates were following their favourite method of silent attack. Two junks, keeping well apart, were secured to each other by a strong rope and when the rope struck the bows of the unsuspecting victim the junks swung into the sides of their catch. The pirates would leap aboard, overcome any opposition, then loot the vessel.

On this occasion, however, when the leaders from each junk leaped aboard *Gnat* they were the ones who received the surprise.

Thanks to Judy's warning the men of the *Gnat* were already strategically placed and the Commanding Officer was directing operations from the bridge. A short burst from the bridge Lewis gun made the message loud and clear—"Pirates go home!"—and as one of the *Gnat*'s seamen cut through the last strands of the rope around *Gnat*'s bows, the pirates scrambled aboard their junks and drifted astern to disappear into the darkness of the night.

Cheers rang out and the Ship's Company decided unanimously that the pirates were frightened off by two things—Judy with her teeth bared, and one of the stokers clad in only the upper half of scarlet pyjamas, who was fiercely waving a Fire Party axe!

Judy's reward came a few days later when she was taken ashore with the shooting party. The shoot was modestly successful, but it was agreed that Judy needed a great deal more training in the art of being a gun-dog.

Not that she didn't try. At one time she stood, perfectly poised, with tail rigid and one fore-paw raised as per manual—but pointing at Tankey!

The Gunboats were not only the smallest ships of the Royal Navy but were quite unlike any other ships on active service. The living accommodation, for example, was the wrong way round, the seamen's messdeck being at the stern, the officers' quarters being in the bow. The two funnels, instead of standing in line, one behind the other, stood side by side behind the bridge. Such arrangements, however, seemed to fit in with the apparent topsy-turviness of the Chinese way of life in which books began on the last page and ended on the first; dinners began with sweets and ended with soup; women wore trousers and men wore long robes; where brides wore red, and white was the colour for mourning.

In such small ships, everyone knew everyone else, intimately, and officers and men worked much more closely together as a team. As each of the Gunboats usually operated alone there were no fleet or flotilla exercises, no endless hoists of signal flags from senior ships, and no critical eyes watching their every movement from flagship bridges.

The Gunboats were always spick and span and highly efficient, but to ensure this the SNO (Senior Naval Officer) would, once or twice a year at short notice, carry out a full-scale "Admiralty Inspection" during which he would not only inspect the ship and the Ship's Company, but also test the efficiency of every man and every department.

A thrill of apprehension ran through the whole Ship's Company when, one morning, the SNO and his Aide were transferred to the *Gnat* to—as Tankey put it—"give them the works".

The SNO inspected the Ship's Company at "Divisions" when the men were lined up on the upper deck. He then inspected their kits and bedding, no item of which—all neatly laid out to show, on each article, the owner's name —escaped his eagle eye.

He paused in front of Judy. She was standing, tongue hanging out and with what appeared to be a huge grin on her face, beside a folded blanket, two neatly-coiled leads, and a spare collar clearly marked "Judy".

With no change of expression, and in complete silence, the SNO moved slowly on to the next seaman.

After inspecting messdecks, store-rooms, stores and engine-room, the two Inspecting Officers returned to the bridge from which vantage point they ordered, and critically observed, every drill and evolution—both known and unknown.

It was like a scene from the Matelots' Inferno. Blocks and tackles and wire ropes seemed to be everywhere. They "Dressed Ship" then lowered the topmast. While the Engineroom Artificers stripped down and then re-assembled the main generator, the order was given to "land armed guard." No sooner had the boat pulled away with the armed guard than it was "man overboard" and "switch on searchlight".

"He'll have to swim until the ruddy boat gets back," muttered one of the scurrying seamen.

Then followed, in succession, "Action Stations," "Fire all guns" and "away kedge anchor".

Tempers were becoming very frayed when Judy decided to set the pattern of her future behaviour and come to the aid of her suffering friends.

On the bridge with the officers, she pointed her nose to the sky and began to bark—furiously and continuously. Just when it looked as if her incessant barking would only succeed in bringing down the wrath of the SNO on to all and sundry, the reason for Judy's barking became evident.

From the point in the sky towards which Judy's nose was pointed appeared a Japanese plane. It swooped low over the Gunboat and then rapidly disappeared into the distance. Only then did Judy stop barking. She turned around as though slowly chasing her own tail then curled up at the feet of the SNO.

Looking from the recumbent Judy to the unsmiling face

of the *Gnat*'s Commanding Officer the much impressed SNO said : "Remarkable. Sound vibrations, presumably, but the time is coming, I think, when we will all need a Judy on the bridge."

As though in agreement that any further activity would be mere anti-climax after Judy's exhibition of do-it-yourself radar, it was decided to call it a day.

The *Gnat* continued on its way up river, destination Hankow where she was to remain for some time. Judy by this time had become an essential member of the crew and, as C.P.O. Jeffery wrote : "She seems to develop a human brain as she gets older. She seems to understand every word. When she gets dirty she comes to me and hangs her head. If I call her a bad dog she drops her ears and then she grins. If I call her a dirty bitch she whines and grovels at my feet. Then I pat her on the head and she knows all is forgiven. Lovely dog."

When the *Gnat* reached Kiu Kiang, C.P.O. Jeffery took Judy to Journey's End, a hotel in a fairly smart town which was a favourite summer holiday spot for the Europeans who could afford it.

"Early one morning I took Judy out for a walk through a wide grassy road with jungle on the left. We walked about a mile and then we turned back towards the hotel. Suddenly Judy left me and darted into the jungle. I knew there were deer about because I'd seen their tracks. I thought she was just having some fun when I heard her yelp. I called her and she came out trembling.

"Before I could touch her she ran ahead of me, keeping to the road. I stopped and looked back and saw in the bush to my right a big leopard. I thought 'That's what frightened Judy'. Only later did I wonder whether Judy had smelt the leopard and distracted its attention so that it wouldn't attack me."

In his diary he wrote : "I shall never know which was the truth."

By now Judy was showing a pattern of behaviour which

was to be repeated again and again in the years ahead—an amazing, uncanny instinct for detecting threatening danger, and an ability to intervene at critical moments when her friends appeared to need help.

# 3 *The Lull Before the Storm*

HANKOW WAS, with its population of more than half a million and its strategic position on the busy Yangtse, a city of considerable size and importance. More than six hundred miles inland from Shanghai, deep in the very heart of China, there were no big hotels, no night-clubs catering for tourists, no super-cinemas. But there was a cinema-cum-theatre which showed only Chinese films and stage shows, and despite warnings from those who had been there before, each Gunboatman would invariably decide to visit it "just this once", the once always turning out to be more than enough.

The welfare of the Gunboatmen, however, was well taken care of at Hankow by the friendliness and the generosity of the officials of the American, British, French, Swiss and German Consulates, their families and staffs.

The largest building on the Hankow Bund (the main street) was the Hong Kong and Shanghai Bank, the ground floor of which had been fitted out as a "wet" canteen and clubroom. Two billiard tables were installed, two English-speaking Chinese boys employed as markers and barmen.

A piano stood on a small stage at one end of the long room. Once a fortnight the men would invite Officers and civilian guests to a "Navy Opera" and sing-song, every such session always ending with the "Yangtse Anthem" which was sung lustily to the combined tunes of

B

"Hallelujah I'm a Bum" and "The More We Are Together".

## STRONG TOPPERS LAMENT

Strong Toppers are we
on the dirty Yangtse
"Gunboats" or "Cruisers"
We're here for a spree.

*Chorus*
Alleluliah Strong Tops
Alleluliah Foxtrots
Alleluliah Strong Toppers
Let's get on with the "Hops"
For the more we are together
Strong Toppers Strong Toppers
For the more we are together
The merrier we shall be.

*Motto*
The more we are together
The merrier we shall be.

Here in their own clubroom the men relaxed, drinking
the strong toppers—Japanese lager-type beer called EWO
and "horsehead", which because of the smell the men felt
sure was made from onions.

To belong to the Strong Toppers Club was a great prize
and the initiation of new members was in itself an evening's entertainment. To win a membership card, the one
on trial had to stand at a table facing three judges.

With a glass of beer in his left hand he then had to
say loudly "Here's to the health of Cardinal Puff", strike
the table once with his right hand, stamp his left foot,
stamp his right foot, tap the glass on the table, then drink
the beer. The sequence would then be repeated but this

time he had to toast the health of Cardinal Puff Puff and tap *twice* with hands and feet. He would then again have to chug-a-lug his beer.

If, up to that point, he had made no mistake in the drill, he would have to do it all a third time but toasting the health of Cardinal Puff Puff Puff and giving three successive taps with feet and hands.

Any mistake, such as grasping the beer glass with the right hand, or the fluffing of lines, would be immediately acclaimed by a roar from the crowd of onlookers—and the unfortunate backslider would have to retire, defeated, or start again from the very beginning.

Judy, naturally—although she liked her beer—didn't have to go through all this. She had a special card fastened to the bulkhead over her bed which was really in recognition of Tankey's determined efforts to make her bark once, then twice, and finally three times in succession.

She was a great favourite with the men and wandered around among them, chewing up the peanuts offered to her, accepting the pats. It was a male world, a world without women, and her presence allowed them to show the long-stored up affection that had little outlet in their way of living.

The *Gnat* was secured alongside Hankow's landing-stage and excursions ashore were frequent. Football and hockey matches were played, often with more zeal than skill.

Judy, of course, took part in every and any activity. Not of much use at football or rugby, she was, however, a force to be reckoned with at hockey. She would scoop up the ball, then streak for goal. As she invariably chose to run to the nearest goal, she scored for both sides with complete impartiality.

The days and weeks slipped by. Judy left her puppy-hood behind and grew into a fine looking animal—sleek and fit and always ready for exercise. The Gunboatmen

decided it was time for her again to try her hand—or paw
—at pointing. After an early breakfast, the party set off—
one Officer, Tankey, four others, and, of course, Judy.

Always pleased to get away from the confines of the
ship, the men and the dog set out jauntily into the open
country beyond Hankow where there was quail in abund-
ance.

The guns barked. The birds fell. As Judy seemed to be
enjoying looking on, the men took turns to use the guns
while the others retrieved the fallen birds. At last Tankey
knelt beside Judy, pointed to a falling bird and said:
"Good girl. Fetch!"

Judy, her head and tail alternately in view as she
bounded through the tall grasses, dashed off in the indicated direction, and disappeared from their sight.

After a long wait and no sign of Judy, the guns were
made "safe" and Tankey went to look for her.

Suddenly he heard a long, heartrending howl. Tankey
had never heard Judy howl before and he ran forward
towards the sound, crashing his way through the grass.
Then he saw her, a picture of utter misery.

She had plunged into a large pool of what appeared to
be wet mud. Such was his haste to reach her that he didn't
even stop to think why she was making no effort to
scramble out.

Tankey was up to his thighs in the dark-brown mess,
and just about alongside Judy when the awful truth was
impressed upon him.

They were standing in an open cess-pit.

The thick dried skin on the surface of the "pool", now
broken by the inrush of their bodies, had been rent apart
to release a sickening paralysing stench. He, too, felt only
capable of just standing there howling in sympathy.

Like a man in a dream—like a man in a nightmare—
his stomach rebelling, his face slightly tinged with green,
Tankey overcame his shocked paralysis, grabbed Judy's
collar and hauled her out behind him.

The revolting mess covered his body. His shoes squelched sickeningly. The slime was on his hands and arms. Judy was even worse off—only her head had escaped the dreadful mush.

Tankey tore off his boots and stockings, grabbed handfuls of grass and rubbed off what he could. He then set to work on Judy, but realised they would have to get back to the *Gnat*, and water.

The other men in the party quickly dispersed at their approach and refused to get within twenty feet of either of them. Too numbed by their disaster to care, Tankey and Judy made their way back to the ship, accompanied by a cloud of excited flies.

As they neared the *Gnat* the first thing Tankey saw was the Q flag blowing in the breeze—the yellow flag that denotes quarantine. The Quartermaster was tolling the ship's bell, chanting "Unclean! Unclean!" It was some days before either Tankey or Judy were considered clean enough to be accepted again as "one of the family".

Early in the spring of 1937, the *Bee*—The Yangtse Flotilla Flagship—arrived at Hankow to relieve the *Gnat*, and for Judy and Vic Oliver it meant a sad parting. They had become good friends since he'd saved her life, and now he was drafted to the *Bee*. He would, of course, see his old shipmates again whenever the *Bee* and the *Gnat* passed each other on the river, or when they both tied up at the same port, but it was, nevertheless, goodbye to their runs ashore together.

In the summer of that year, the Japanese really went to war against the Chinese peoples, without the formality of a declaration. One night in July, near Peking, the Japanese troops on night exercises and manoeuvres, clashed with Chinese soldiers near the Marco Polo bridge. Shots were exchanged and soldiers on both sides were hit.

The Japanese then demanded the withdrawal of all Chinese forces from the area, and issued an ultimatum.

When the Chinese ignored the ultimatum the Japanese launched a violent attack in that area and bombed Tientsin.

On August 9th another clash between Chinese and Japanese near Shanghai provided the excuse for which the Japanese had been waiting. The Japanese bombarded Woosung, landed a large naval party at Shanghai—and the war was on, a savage, ruthless, one-sided war.

By November of that year the Chinese were on the retreat, fleeing along the valley of the Yangtse pursued by more than ninety thousand Japanese.

It was during this month that the *Gnat* called in to Nanking and found herself in the company of the American Gunboat USS *Panay*. A friendship was made and the two ship's companies welcomed each other to their canteens.

One evening Judy went with Tankey to the shore canteen and soon the beer was flowing and songs were being sung with the strength of sail and shanty days.

The Americans loved Judy and she was made the centre of attraction. They loved the way she enthusiastically added her whine to the men's noisy renderings, and showered affection on her.

Eventually the party came to an end and Tankey reluctantly wished everyone good night and returned to *Gnat*. Only when he had boarded her did he realise that Judy was not at his heels.

Tankey sobered immediately and organised a search party. They looked everywhere but there was no sign. A signal was flashed to *Panay* asking if they'd seen Judy and the *Gnat*'s company were even more despondent when the reply came back : "Sorry no trace of her here."

It was a bad night for everybody. Tankey was sad at heart, blaming himself for not keeping an eye on her. He slept little but his tiredness disappeared next morning when he heard through the grapevine of the Chinese Boatboys that Judy *was* aboard *Panay*.

"So that's how they're playing it," said Tankey, and laid his plans.

When darkness came a sampan crept quietly alongside *Panay*, watching, waiting for the moment when the decks were clear. Two men crept on board, there were hushed words, and then they returned to the sampan.

The following morning came a signal from Panay :

TO *GNAT* : BOARDED AT NIGHT BY PIRATES. SHIP'S BELL STOLEN. *GNAT* TO *PANAY* : *WE* ALSO PIRATED—OF JUDY. WILL SWOP ONE BELL BELONGING TO USS *PANAY* FOR ONE LADY NAMED JUDY PROPERTY OF OFFICERS AND SHIP'S COMPANY OF HMS *GNAT*.

Within the hour Judy was back on board the *Gnat* and the *Panay*'s quarterdeck was once more graced by the ship's bell. No one but no one was going to part Judy and the Royal Navy.

Just weeks later Nanking was captured and it was estimated that more than ten thousand Chinese—men, women and children—were killed. The Great Powers, led by Great Britain and America, sent strong notes of protest. The Japanese replied with the then comparatively new but highly successful form of warfare, mass bombing.

This was a very difficult time for the Gunboats. British and foreign ships were being attacked and boarded as the Japanese tried to bring the river traffic to a halt. Their plans were foiled by the introduction of small convoys under the direct guardianship of British and American gunboats.

It was in December that the Japanese attacked the gunboats. First HMS *Ladybird* which was at Wuhu watching over a number of British steamers busily unloading and loading cargoes.

The Japanese attack with bombs and machine guns was

unexpected, brief, but successful. One of the steamers sank and another was badly damaged.

*Ladybird's* wireless signal to the Senior Naval Officer on the *Bee* at Hankow brought the *Bee* steaming down river, but too late to prevent another attack on the *Ladybird,* this time by shore batteries.

The *Ladybird* was hit again and again at almost point-blank range.

Sick Berth Attendant Terence Lonergan was killed; all the officers and a Petty Officer Smallwood were injured.

At Nanking, the two British Gunboats, *Scarab* and *Cricket,* were in company with a group of British steamers when they were attacked by Japanese dive-bombers. The Gunboats were, however, now very much on the alert, and the bombers were met by such a concentrated fury of anti-aircraft fire that they were forced to turn away after dropping their bombs at random.

The same day the Japanese turned their attention on the Americans, on the Gunboat USS *Panay* which only weeks earlier had been a scene of joy and merriment.

Acting as escort to a group of Standard Oil Company ships and lighters, the *Panay* at the time was practically a floating Embassy, with a number of Consular officials and newspaper reporters on board.

There was no warning; no time for defensive measures.

The Japanese bombers suddenly appeared to dive, bomb and machine-gun the little ships. Every ship in the small convoy was hit. The *Panay,* under a hail of bombs, heeled over and sank.

Bad news, in this particular instance, did not travel fast. When Admiral Yarnell, Commander-in-Chief of the US Asiatic Fleet, could not contact the *Panay* by wireless he asked the *Bee,* then at Wuhu with the damaged *Ladybird,* to locate the *Panay* and report back to him at Shanghai.

The *Bee,* accompanied by the *Ladybird,* soon discovered why there had been no messages from the *Panay*—and why there would be no more. Ships and lighters, some still burning, were lying, half submerged, along the river banks.

There was no sign of life until two Americans appeared on the river bank, shouting and waving. When they reported that the remainder, including the many wounded, were at a Chinese village some twenty miles inland, a force of unarmed sailors were put ashore with orders to bring back all survivors.

The rescue was completed without further incident, but the wireless report to Admiral Yarnell shocked even the world's news editors.

The *Panay* had been sunk. Two naval ratings had been killed. Three officers and eight ratings were seriously injured. Two officers and twenty-seven ratings were wounded. An Italian journalist had been killed.

Reaction from both Governments—British and American—was immediate. They demanded some millions of dollars as compensation, the removal of the Japanese Colonel responsible for the attacks, and a pledge that attacks on shipping should cease. Their demands were met and the Gunboats continued to carry out their patrol duties, making great effort to avoid causing "incidents".

There were "incidents", of course. The Gunboatmen had made many friends among the Chinese people along the Yangtse, and their sympathies were with the Chinese in their struggle to prevent Japanese domination. Short of any action that could be construed as being provocative, the Gunboatmen leaned over backwards to assist the Chinese in any way possible. When the families in their riverboat homes asked to be tied up to the Gunboats for safety they were never refused.

Such sympathetic action often led to a form of confrontation. Following an exchange of notes, the local Japanese Commanding Officer would be received aboard the offending Gunboat. Trailing a sword much too big for him, he would be ceremoniously piped aboard to be greeted by the Gunboat Captain and escorted to the Captain's quarters.

Gunboat Captains, however, were themselves very competent diplomats and the visiting Japanese officer would eventually depart, evidently mollified and, even more evidently, full of wardroom rum.

For Judy, too, that year, 1938, was to be full of "incidents".

# 4 *Judy Becomes a Mother*

To MAINTAIN the Gunboats in a constant condition of
fighting efficiency, some of the crew of each Gunboat were
relieved, each year, by men sent out from England to serve
their turn of "foreign service"—a period of from two to
two and a half years.

In 1938 it was the turn of Judy's four best friends—
Chief Bosun's mate Charles Jeffery who had found Judy
for the navy; Vic Oliver, the Leading Seaman who had
fished her out of the river; Chief Sick Berth Attendant
Bill Wilson who looked after her general health ("I
sometimes gave her a dose of Syrup of Buckthorn")
and Jan Cooper (Tankey) who tried hard to teach her
to point—to leave the China Station for England and
home.

Judy had not yet found one master and extended her
friendship to everyone alike. However, when the new
arrivals from England boarded the *Gnat* at Shanghai she
immediately "adopted" two of them—Leading Seaman
Law, a huge, pleasant young man, and Able Seaman Boni-
face better known as Bonny.

When the *Gnat* again tied up at Hankow the city was
much changed. The Chinese, preparing to defend it
against the still advancing Japanese, were building air raid
shelters, throwing up defensive earthworks.

During the Gunboat's stay in Hankow Judy had made

three Chinese friends. Because they were very fond of
Judy, they deserve mention in her story.

Wherever sailors are found together in large numbers,
there, too, will be found a man—usually a shopkeeper,
a tailor or a publican—who will be looked up on by
them as a friend, banker, and father confessor.

In Plymouth it was "Tubby" Greenburgh, a fat, jolly,
naval tailor from whom the sailors could always borrow
ten shillings on "blank" weeks—interest free, and only
made binding by a handshake.

In Wei Hai Wei it was "Jelly Belly", a huge man who,
as the men from the visiting fleet poured ashore for leave
or recreation, boomed at, and beamed on, his prodigal
sons, and who gave away more of the fresh fruit on his
stall than he sold.

Joe Binks—one of Judy's friends at Hankow—was such
a man. His real name was Sung, but he was affectionately
known to all and sundry as Joe Binks. The official ships'
compradore at Hankow, he was responsible for the food
and other supplies the ships needed. When he arrived on
board he was sometimes accompanied by his wife and four
children—much to Judy's delight.

Joe Binks was the proud possessor of a decoration which
had been pinned to his chest by a representative of HM
Government in recognition of his devotion to duty many
years before, when, despite threats from other suppliers,
he continued to supply HM ships during a major anti-
British campaign.

"Sew-sew", another of Judy's friends, was a woman—a
gentle soft-spoken, doe-eyed woman who was allowed on
board to do any necessary sewing repairs to clothing or
equipment. A skilled needlewoman, she would sit on the
end of a messdeck stool, busily attaching new white tapes
to a uniform collar and talking, in a soft sing-song voice,
to an enraptured Judy.

Amah, the third of Judy's friends, was also a woman
but made of much sterner stuff. She was the head of a

young family all of whom lived in their small rattan-covered sampan. Paid by the Admiralty, she had bargained for, and obtained, the right to be used as the Gunboats' "general use" boat. She would cheerfully transport men from ship to river bank or, just as cheerfully, paint the ship's side from the platform of her floating home.

Judy loved her and her family and she would sometimes jump down into the sampan to play with the children. It was their loud squeals of delight that always warned Bonny of the wayward Judy's whereabouts.

Also at Hankow at that time there were two other Gunboats—one American, one French. The presence of the French Gunboat was to have a tremendous impact on Judy—and it all began when Bonny was sitting at the mess-deck table writing a letter to his girl-friend in Portsmouth.

Deep in concentration Bonny became aware that Judy seemed unusually active. She would get to her feet, whine, then lay down again. A few minutes later up she got again, walked to the ladder which led to the upper deck, looked imploringly towards Bonny, then returned to squat between his feet.

Bonny put down his pen in despair.

"How," he said, "can I persuade my barmaid in the Air Balloon that it would be all right for us to go on holiday together without her Mum if you keep on moaning and fidgeting?"

Judy walked over to the foot of the messdeck ladder.

"What's up with you, anyhow? Do you want to go for a little walk? Go on then—up you go."

He followed Judy up the ladder to the upper deck, down the short gangway and on to the hulk. Surprisingly—or so it seemed to Bonny—she showed no desire to play. Head held high, tail straight out, she trotted sedately up and down the hulk.

Bonny looked across to where, on the other side of the hulk, the French Gunboat, the *Francis Garnier*, was secured—and then began to understand Judy's apparently strange behaviour.

On the bridge of the *Francis Garnier*, watching her every movement, stood a dog that was broader of chest, slightly bigger than Judy, but nevertheless almost a replica of the lovely animal.

Bonny watched as Judy trotted unconcernedly up the gangway of the *Gnat* and disappeared down through the messdeck hatch.

"Well, I'm damned," murmured Bonny. "So that's why she was so fidgety. But how like a female—she must have known he was there yet she didn't even look at him, just showed herself off : then disappeared."

The *Francis Garnier's* dog, Paul, was, like Judy, a pedigree pointer, but, unlike Judy, he made no secret that for him it was love at first sight. Whenever he saw Judy he acted like a dog with six legs and no brains. Right in front of his lady-love, he sprawled in a most undignified manner, down the ship's gangway. He galloped about on the hulk like a metal-clad war-horse, seemingly unaware of Judy's coyness and occasionally snapping teeth.

Then one day, in a boastful attempt to show off his prowess, Paul tore along the full length of the metal hulk at full speed, only to find, too late, that he could not stop. With a despairing howl, and a mighty splash, Paul went over the side.

Judy, no longer unconcerned, sprang to the edge of the hulk barking loudly and urgently. Bonny, however, was already at hand to kneel beside Judy and to haul the bedraggled Paul on to the hulk. Judy licked his face, whined, nuzzled against him, and pawed him. For Paul further duckings were unnecessary. The fate of the two pointers was in the hands of the Ship's Companies of the *Gnat* and the *Francis Garnier*.

Sailors are strange animals—amiable, lovable and with an absurd sense of humour which has to be experienced to be understood. In a world without women where discipline and authority are paramount, they find their own ways of letting off steam. They play silly games like "Uckers"—the navy version of Ludo—where instead of a board, a huge piece of painted canvas, about six feet square, is laid on the deck. The coloured playing pieces or "Uckers"—with which one hopes to "Uck off" one's opponents—are about eight inches in diameter. The dice —huge wooden cubes—are shaken in, and thrown from, a bucket.

While this may sound passably entertaining, the amazing feature of the game is that all the players must dress in fancy dress—as a vicar, a duchess, an admiral, a Hottentot, or any other character, depending on the imagination of the individual or on the variety of costumes in the ship's amateur theatrical locker.

"Messdeck Gunnery," another favourite game, is less bizarre but equally as entertaining, and has the advantage of not requiring any "props'.

A bored messdeck will suddenly be galvanised into frantic activity by a sudden yell of "gun's crew close up !" The number of men required to man and operate a six-inch gun will line up and "number" as others move tables and stools to provide a space in which the "crew" can operate.

At the command "Commence firing" the crew swings into action, action in which every drill and operation of a genuine six-inch gun's crew is faithfully carried out in detail.

The nearest port-hole (the breech) is flung open. The "shell" is then pushed out, the "gun" is fired, and the bottom of an upturned zinc bath is given a mighty thump with a huge wooden mallet.

Woe to the luckless man who has left his "scrub deck" boots under the table, or who has stuffed his old scarf behind the mess cups. To the hungry hands of the "loader" anything within reach is "ammunition".

In the light of this knowledge of off-duty activity the

subsequent behaviour of the men of both ships where Judy's love life was concerned can be more readily understood.

On the afternoon of Paul's ducking, five men of the *Gnat* sat around the messdeck table on which, wearing her best collar, sat Judy.

"We feel," began Bonny, "that the time has come when we should have a serious talk. We are, so to speak, your legal guardians, and we naturally want to do our best for your happiness, but everything must be done properly and according to the rules."

Judy, her head cocked on one side, was as usual all attention—but without understanding. Nevertheless she licked his hand as though to reassure him.

"Paul," continued Bonny, "is a very nice dog, with a pedigree too, and they are a very nice bunch on the *Francis Garnier*, so you can get engaged today, and married tomorrow—and we'll call your first pup Bonny."

The Ship's Electrician raised one of Judy's paws and slipped over it a small anklet which had been designed and made for the occasion.

"And that," he said, "is your engagement ring."

The next day, immediately after lunch, Judy and Paul were led out on to the centre of the hulk so that both crews could watch the ceremony.

Bonny, with his "opposite number"—the Tankey from the *Francis Garnier*—officiated. Watched by the applauding men of both crews and by a small group of wondering Chinese, Bonny patted both dogs on the head as he announced, "I pronounce thee—" then looked around at the circle of grinning faces as though for inspiration, "Dog and bitch?" "Paul and Judy?"

Only a Frenchman could have solved the problem so neatly. The First Lieutenant of the *Francis Garnier* called out from his vantage point on the bridge—"One!"

And so Paul and Judy were married.

Paul remained on the *Gnat* for three days, sharing a

specially-built "love nest", and was then returned, pro-
testing loudly, to his own ship.

The weeks went by and Judy grew bigger and plumper;
her big brown eyes even more soulful with the new
responsibilities she was preparing for. Then, one morning
during the time the Japanese bombers had begun their
daily attacks, Bonny slid down the ladder to the Seamen's
messdeck.

A tired, unshaven, but triumphant Bonny.

"They're here!" he yelled. "Thirteen of them!"

No one on that ship thought that he was referring to
the bombers and they queued to see the thirteen naked,
tiny pups in Judy's basket. Three of them, weaker than
the others, died, but the remaining ten puppies waxed
fat.

Judy didn't seem to mind the constant stream of viewers
and well-wishers who were always making excuses to go
aboard the *Gnat* to see the pups. Paul, however, was not
allowed to see his offspring until Judy and the waddling
little pups were able to exercise on the hulk, each on a
separate lead.

As the weeks went by, the pups grew more and more
venturesome. There were times when the *Gnat* seemed to
be swarming with pups. Wherever one looked, there would
be a pup. They galloped about on fat little legs. They
chewed anything within their reach. They made incredibly
—impossibly—large puddles.

It was time, decided the *Gnat*'s Commanding Officer,
to make the inevitable decision. The pups had to go.

The withdrawal of Judy's pups was gradual. First choice
went to the officers and men of the *Francis Garnier*, who
had the pick of the litter. Officials of the Hankow Race
Club asked for one of the pups, offering, in exchange, one
Lewis gun and four pans of ammunition which was
accepted by the Commanding Officer of the *Gnat*, not
merely as a fee but because it was realised that the arrival

of the Japanese in Hankow could well cause trouble to any person possessing arms.

Some pups were given to Consular officials and their families, one to an American Gunboat *Guam*. The last went about two months later to a Scottish Engineer on one of the river steamers.

The bombing attacks on Hankow increased, both in number and ferocity, and it was again evident that the Japanese were prepared to show open hostility to any of the Great Powers, if and when it suited their purpose.

One morning, soon after the birth of Judy's pups, a group of Japanese bombers approached Hankow along the river valley.

A huge Union Jack was painted on the *Gnat*'s awnings but the leading bomber ignored it and released two bombs, both of which dropped into the river some distance ahead of the Gunboat. Quite unprepared for the unwarranted attack, the Gunboatmen moved to Action Stations.

Suddenly overhead there was the sound of Chinese fighter planes and another Yangtse "incident" was avoided. The planes had obviously been waiting high above Hankow and they swooped down on the Japanese bombers, destroying two of them and sending the remainder scuttling for base.

These Chinese planes, manned by a mixed crowd of Chinese, Russian, British and American fliers, were, at that time a real problem to the Japanese Bomber Command. They couldn't understand how they always knew when an attack was imminent.

Had the men of the *Gnat* known then about the way the Chinese fighters were alerted they would undoubtedly have made two medals, each as big as a dustbin lid, one for an American woman doctor named Hyla S. Watters, and the other for their own Telegraphist Stanley Cotterrall.

Stanley Cotterrall, had, some months earlier, been landed at the American Mission Hospital, Wuhu, to undergo an urgent operation. The operation was followed by a second, then a third. Dr. Watters had been the surgeon.

Let her explain how they came to help the men further up the river.

"It all began when a Chinese boy was carried into the hospital at Wuhu after being badly wounded by bandits.

"Needing another doctor to help me in an immediate operation, I decided to send our Chinese driver down to the Wuhu loading stage in the hospital car to try to get a message to a ship which was lying at anchor some little way down river.

"Stanley Cotterrall, a Telegraphist from HMS *Gnat*, who had been in my hospital for nearly six months and on whom I had operated for the third time only that very morning, called out from his bed. 'What's the point of having a Telegraphist here if you don't make use of him? Get someone to carry me up on the roof, then bring me a good light and I'll make a signal for you.'

"With some misgivings about moving him so soon after his operation we did carry him up on to the roof from where he sent a signal which brought a doctor.

"My mother, who was at the hospital with me, said, 'Why depend on having a sick Telegraphist in hospital? Get him to teach you how to signal then you can make the signals yourself.'

"It was a good idea, and Stanley started to teach me the morse code. I persuaded some of the young men on the hospital staff to also join the class but after a little while they appeared to lose interest.

"Later on I found out that they had secretly continued to learn not only morse but radio, so that they could send signals to warn the Chinese Air Force in Hankow when Japanese bombers flew westward over the hospital.

"During the Japanese occupation, but before Pearl Harbour, the Japanese caught me signalling to one of the Ship's doctors. It could easily have been the end of me, but when they tested my rhythm they found that I was not the mysterious sender of radio signals for whom they were searching. I didn't know, then, that some of my own staff were responsible.

"I am now living in New York. The two young doctors who worked with me at Wuhu, Paul and Stella Sommerfreund, are now living and practising in Canada."

# 5 A New Assignment

DURING 1938 Chiang Kai-Shek transferred his head-quarters to Hankow, but still the Japanese advance along the Yangtse valley continued. The Chinese fled before the Japanese hordes, hordes which perpetrated the most appalling war crimes of modern times.

Thousands of Chinese—men, women and children—were added to the death roll. Hundreds of swollen corpses were swept down and along the Great River.

The men of the Gunboats, angry and sick at heart, were powerless to help. They could only continue their patrols, protecting as they did so Consulates, banks, business houses, and the shipping on the river. Had the League of Nations acted then, how different could have been the progress of the war in Europe, a war which was even then starting to cast its shadows across the Western World.

In August the *Gnat* took part in a particularly hazardous rescue operation, described here by C.P.O. Jim Mills, who was on the Gunboat in 1938 and 39.

"A Customs vessel, the *Chianghsing*, had been moving the river marker buoys in order to make it more difficult for the advance of Japanese troops. They were observed from the air and bombed.

"Sinking and on fire, the *Chianghsing* was rammed into the river bank and abandoned. Officers and crew suc-ceeded in getting ashore but were then machine gunned.

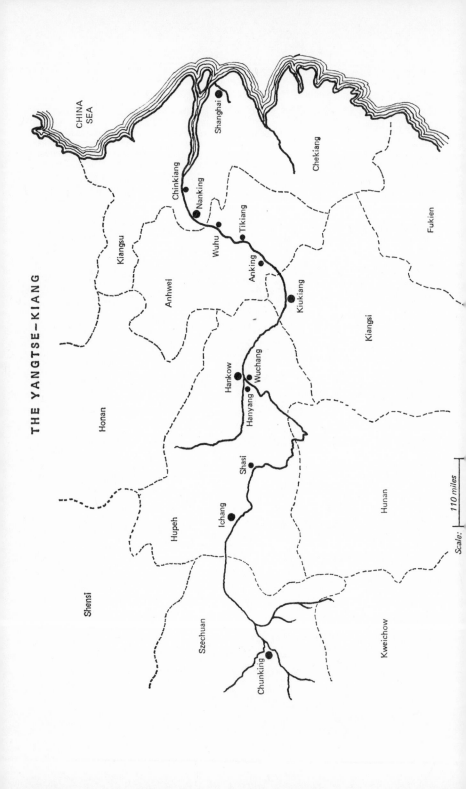

THE YANGTSE–KIANG

The Captain—Captain Crowley—the First Officer, and the Engineer were killed and other crew members were wounded.

"When the *Gnat* arrived on the scene a Japanese plane was still buzzing around. Hoping that the huge Union Jack on our awning would mean something to the pilot, we lowered two boats and brought aboard the survivors, the wounded and the dead."

A month later the men on the *Gnat* received two footballs—"A small and most inadequate token of the thanks and appreciation of the few members of the Custom staff here most closely connected with the *Chianghsing* and those who were killed in her," wrote E. N. Enson from Hankow.

"You British navy men, whatever your rank, are invariably and cheerfully ready to go to the help of anyone whoever they may be. Although you regarded this trip as just part of the day's work, your attempt to pass off a very gallant act as a mere bit of routine work does not diminish in the least the feelings of respect and gratitude with which we civilians regard you."

Times were critical but as Mills wrote, "Life wasn't all tragedy." He remembers with pleasure the shore canteen at Wuhu where the Gunboatmen met, drank and made merry.

"Ice-cream was also available and as soon as we entered Judy was always given a big plateful. One evening when no one remembered to get it for her, she went behind the bar and dragged out the huge carton into the centre of the room.

"She went with us everywhere. While at Nanking we arranged a visit to Sun Yat Sen's tomb but because of a shortage of cars, we were provided with five cars and a big glass-sided hearse. Everyone made a dash for the cars leaving five of us, and Judy, to travel in the hearse.

"What the others didn't know was that all the beer had been put into the hearse. We not only had the best view on the way to the tomb but we must have been the merriest passengers that the hearse had ever carried."

That shore canteen must have indeed been something if a man will take on the notorious river to reach it. "Duggie" Gower was duty Quartermaster on the *Ladybird* one night when the ship's company went to the canteen. Tired of being left out of all the fun, he strapped his ukelele to his back and slipped down the tow rope. With no buoyancy in the water he went straight under. He had about 100 yards to go and it took him a long time of dog paddling to get there. Covered in mud, his ukelele missing, he had time for just one beer before everyone returned to their ships. Gower, having left without permission, had to be smuggled back on board. Judy, Gower and Wugle were the only three known to have come out of the Yangtse alive.

In October of 1938 the Japanese forces entered Hankow, and it was at Hankow that Judy came up against the same anger she experienced as a pup.

She had been taken ashore by Bonny and Leading Seaman Law for her usual daily exercise and they were returning to the *Gnat*. As they passed one of the many Japanese sentries who were posted on the waterfront, Judy, in her usual friendly fashion, trotted over to him, and in the way of all dogs, lowered her head to sniff at his boots. Reaction was swift and unexpected. His voice rising to a frienzied scream, the sentry raged at Judy and at the two seamen. The dog did not move. Instead she raised her eyes to his angry face, then curled back her lip in a silent snarl.

The sentry stepped back a pace, aimed his rifle at Judy's head, opened the bolt and closed it, thus putting one bullet in the breech ready to fire.

There was no doubt in the minds of Judy's two companions that he would fire it, and so end the Judy story there and then.

Leading Seaman Law didn't *need* time to think—he swept the sentry, still holding his rifle and still screaming abuse, up in his mighty arms and heaved him into the river.

Stopping only long enough to see the sentry crawl to the river bank, the men, followed by Judy, hurried aboard to report the incident.

During the next few days there were many comings and goings to and from the *Gnat*. Local Japanese Commanding Officers were piped aboard almost daily in their investigation of the alleged rough treatment to one of the Japanese liberators and many signal messages were sent and received by the Commanding Officer of the *Gnat*.

No one ever really knew what was said but from that time on Judy remained on board. She had had her last run ashore at Hankow.

By 1938 the Gunboats were all old ships. They had seen service in World War I and some had been continuously in service, except for periodical refits, since the turn of the century. The Admiralty decided to replace them with bigger and more up-to-date Gunboats, and in December the first of them, HMS *Scorpion,* appeared on the Yangtse to take over from the *Bee* as the flagship of the Rear Admiral Yangtse. Some months later, came two more —HMS *Grasshopper* and HMS *Dragonfly*.

The *Bee* and the *Mantis* were condemned as being past repair and both ships were sent to Shanghai to be sold as scrap.

In June of the next year part of the *Gnat*'s ship's company were transferred to the *Grasshopper* and Judy went with them.

The Gunboats continued to patrol the river but when war was declared on Germany in September of that year, the Admiralty moved the pieces on the huge naval chessboard and signalled the withdrawal of the Gunboats from the Great River.

The *Gnat, Ladybird, Cockchafer, Cricket,* and *Tarantula* all followed the *Scorpion, Dragonfly* and *Grasshopper* to Singapore.

The *Gannet, Falcon* and *Sandpiper* remained, and were handed over to the Chinese Government.

The *Cicala, Tern, Moth* and *Robin*, all from the West River and based on Canton, were eventually sent to Hong Kong.

When the *Grasshopper* steamed, for the last time, away from Shanghai, Judy, for the first time in her young life, left China and the confines of the Yangtse River.

Judy, on a strange ship, with many new shipmates, sailing away from the *Gnat*, her home for some three years, and from her many friends along the river, now had a new misery to contend with—seasickness.

On the long sea trip the *Grasshopper* rolled, heaved and slewed.

Her new friends, however, although sympathetic, were firm. They could not force her to eat, but they could force her to take exercise and this they did. Before their arrival at Hong Kong, Judy had found her sea legs and was eating, so the Coxswain said, like a horse.

Judy was never seasick again and, by the time that the *Grasshopper*, in company with the *Dragonfly*, arrived at Singapore, Judy was back to her old self again.

The two Gunboats, because they were on active service at a large naval base, had a different way of life and routines from those which the men enjoyed when they operated as independent units on the Yangtse river.

Singapore itself, far from any battlefront, appeared to live by the slogan "business—and pleasure—as usual," and the Gunboatmen, when ashore, were able to relax and enjoy themselves in a pleasure-loving city remote and somewhat aloof from the war that was then raging in Europe.

For Judy it was certainly a happy and carefree period—carefree, until the morning when she met up with an animal that was beyond her understanding. She had been away from the ship for a week staying with a Customs official whose three children adored her.

On the morning of her return to the ship, as Judy leaped joyfully up the gangway, everyone was watching to see her reactions—as one of stokers said : "This should be worth seeing."

A length of wire had been secured along part of the upper deck so that it stretched tautly at a height of about four feet. Attached to the wire by a metal ring so that the ring could slide freely along the wire was a long lead and on the end of that lead was a monkey.

As Judy trotted on to the upper deck, the monkey sprang and landed firmly astride Judy's back where he clung with both arms and legs like a miniature jockey.

Judy leaped, bucked, cavorted—but the monkey remained firmly attached until Judy, puzzled and defeated, did what any female would do—she sat down and howled.

The monkey, as though sorry for his unwarranted behaviour, slid from Judy's back and endeavoured to put one arm around her neck. But Judy, her mind working clearly again, edged her way along the deck until she was able to leap down through the messdeck hatch.

The monkey—Mickey—had been offered a "temporary" home on the *Grasshopper* when his previous owners had sailed for the Persian Gulf a few days earlier. Someone was always going to release it in Malaya, but somehow no one ever actually got around to doing it.

Judy neither ignored it nor tried to get friendly with it. It would sometimes again leap on her back to be carried, jockey fashion, along the limits of the wire, but if Judy suffered she suffered in silence.

She was, however, to get some pleasure out of Mickey.

A few days later a man, wearing the uniform of a Petty Officer with, on one arm, the badge of a Coxswain, strode up the *Grasshopper*'s gangway.

Petty Officer George White was reporting aboard his

new ship. He saluted as he stepped from the gangway on
to the upper deck—then almost fell to his knees in surprise
as a hurtling Mickey landed on his shoulders and whipped
off his cap.

But Mickey was no match for the strong hands of the
Petty Officer. The cap was wrenched from the monkey's
hands, and Mickey, screaming his protest, was dumped
unceremoniously on the deck as the Petty Officer stepped
rather smartly out of range.

As he replaced his cap on his head, Petty Officer White
saw Judy. She was sitting, herself out of reach of the leap-
ing Mickey and it seemed to him that she was "laughing
her silly head off."

On the day Petty Officer White reported on board the
*Grasshopper*, other men, newly arrived at Singapore from
England, were joining other ships.

One of them, Leading Stoker Les Searle, was reporting
to the Officer of the Watch on the *Dragonfly*, the *Grasshopper*'s sister ship. He, too, was to play an important
part in the Judy story.

The year 1941 saw the forces of Great Britain and the
Commonwealth stretched to the very limits of their re-
sources in Europe, the Mediterranean and the Middle East.
In the Far East there were ominous signs that the Japanese
were planning further expansion, and this was emphasised,
in July, when the Japanese occupied Saigon in Indo-China
from where they could control the whole of the China
Seas.

The Admiralty, always aware of the possibility of Japan
seizing the chance to bid for complete domination of the
Far East while Great Britain was so fully committed in
the West, had in hand a tentative plan whereby the French
fleet would take over in the Mediterranean, freeing British
ships for bases at Colombo or Singapore.

With the European war going so badly in France, the
use of the French fleet had been denied to the British. The
Americans, although already doing everything in their

power to help, would not necessarily come into the war if, as seemed likely, Japan should declare war on the Allies. So, in the hope of deterring the Japanese from further acts of aggression, two British battleships—HMS *Repulse* and HMS *Prince of Wales*—were sent to bolster the naval strength based on Singapore.

In Singapore itself the defences were being strengthened —while the Japanese residents, many of whom were employed by British officials, continued to smile blandly as, each morning, they greeted their employers with deference. Few of the Japanese employees belonged to the tennis clubs or bridge clubs, but they all carried cameras, they all took note, and notes and they all wore—as did the tiger —an enigmatic smile, the reason for which was very soon to be made apparent.

The Japanese invaded Siam (Thailand) and so positioned their forces on the very threshold of Malaya. The stage was set for the final act in the drama which was to result in the fall of Singapore—and the end of the Gunboats.

The curtain went up on the final act at eight o'clock on the morning of Sunday, December 7th, when planes from six Japanese aircraft carriers attacked the United States Pacific Fleet at Pearl Harbor.

In less than thirty minutes practically the whole of the American battle fleet was wiped out, and all hope of retaining control of the South West Pacific and the China Sea went with it. Japanese forces attacked Hong Kong and the Philippines, and landed troops on Malaya—Singapore was well and truly in the war.

The first wave of bombers to be aimed at Singapore never arrived. Instead they caught the two battleships, *Repulse* and the *Prince of Wales*, at sea without air cover and sank them both.

On the 25th, Christmas Day, Hong Kong surrendered to the Japanese, leaving Singapore as the next obvious target.

During the next eight weeks the British and Allied forces fought to stem the advance of the Japanese to Malaya, but were forced to retreat ever southwards until, in Singapore itself, the last stand was made.

Those eight weeks were very hectic for the *Grasshopper*, the *Dragonfly* and the *Scorpion*. Although, because of the Japanese superiority both at sea and in the air, they were mostly limited to night operations, they were here, there, and everywhere. They bombarded the coastline of Malaya to give covering fire to retreating allied troops, and were often called upon to evacuate isolated pockets of men from difficult situations..

When the *Grasshopper*'s guns opened up, Judy didn't panic or cry or howl; she just stuck it out like the rest of the Gunboat's crew.

She was, though, an invaluable and reliable early warning system—barking in the right direction before the enemy planes appeared. She could also be replied upon to keep quiet when it was really necessary for silence to be maintained—for example when the Gunboats were stealthily, in the darkness of the night, attempting to rescue battered remnants of an Indian Division from the Malayan coast.

It was after such an expedition that a firm friendship was struck between Judy and Les Searle. Leading Stoker Searle, three other ratings from the *Dragonfly*, and an officer, were, one night, put ashore on the Malayan coast to try to make contact with a group of Sappers whose retreat southwards towards Singapore had been cut off by advancing Japanese.

Had Judy been with them, she would have warned them of the proximity of the enemy, but they had no warning until a bullet from the darkness tore through the leg of Les Searle. The five men returned safely to their ship, and on their return to Singapore Les Searle was taken ashore to the naval hospital and with the *Grasshopper*'s Sick Berth Attendant, Judy became a frequent visitor. Les

Searle had heard of, and had seen Judy before but it was only then that they became really close friends.

Judy wasn't to know it, but, at that time, the one man for whom she had been waiting—her future master—was only a mile away, in Singapore, and he, too, would soon be preparing to leave.

# 6 *Flight From Singapore*

"From the Yangtse River Gunboats
Only one in ten returned
When the Little Ships Flotilla
Off Malaya redly burned.
The jungled isles fell silent
And the heaving water sighed
As the women and the children
And the sailors rudely died."*

WHEN SINGAPORE, so often described as the Impregnable Fortress and the Gibraltar of the East, fell it was also the end of the long history of Gunboat activity in the Far East.

British sea power east of the Indian Ocean practically ceased to exist. With the sinking of the two great warships *Repulse* and *Prince of Wales* it was left to the three Gunboats, *Scorpion, Dragonfly* and *Grasshopper,* some submarines and a few other even smaller vessels, to uphold the finest traditions of the Royal Navy.

All based on Singapore, they were, in January and early February of 1942 continuously in demand to assist the movements of British and Commonwealth troops as the Japanese pressed ever southward in Malaya. But the activities of the litle ships were becoming more and more limited

* From *The Little Ships Flotilla,* by Edwin Varley

by the Japanese advances on land and the overwhelming superiority of the Japanese forces at sea and in the air.

Under ceaseless bombing and shelling, Singapore was being reduced to a shambles. Crowded with refugees from the mainland, retreating troops, fighting men separated from their units, deserters and looters, co-ordinated resistance was more and more impossible.

Rumour followed rumour—the water supply had been destroyed; the Japanese were taking no prisoners; every man for himself—and the chaos was intensified. Dockyard installations and the big harbour guns had already been destroyed by the Naval personnel. The oil storage tanks had all been fired. As the thick black clouds from the blazing oil tanks spread over the docks and city, blanketing the smoke from the many fires already raging there, it seemed to be the final admission that the end was now in sight.

Still there was a blind belief that another "Miracle of Dunkirk" would naturally materialise, and that the Royal Navy would again scoop everyone to safety. But it was painfully apparent to those who had eyes to see, that, with the tiny Naval force available, there could now be no large-scale withdrawal from Singapore.

On January 30th, in a convoy which had included the SS *Duchess of Bedford,* four thousand women and children were evacuated. A few days later, the *Empress of Asia* which was carrying relief troops to Singapore was bombed and sunk.

By February 11th the *Grasshopper* and *Dragonfly* were the biggest ships in the remaining fleet of fifty little ships, many of which were not only unarmed but had up to that time been used as steamers.

Rear-Admiral E. J. Spooner had asked, and been given permission to order the departure from Singapore of all the remaining little ships. Between them they would carry nearly three thousand passengers and would be the last to leave the doomed city.

The *Scorpion,* already damaged by air attacks on the

C

10th, was one of the first of the little ships to leave. She was also one of the first to die. On the thirteenth—Friday the thirteenth—*Scorpion* passed through the Berhala Strait, nearly seventy miles south of Singapore. Off Berhala Island a Japanese cruiser and two destroyers were sighted and all four ships opened fire immediately. The relatively tiny Gunboat had no chance. Out of control, blazing from stem to stern, she was abandoned. Moments later the *Scorpion* went down. Only three Carley floats could be launched, and there were twenty survivors, all picked up by the Japanese.

One of those who died was Chief Petty Officer Charles Goodyear who, when serving in the Gunboat HMS *Bee*, had been a close friend of Vic Oliver and Judy. Both had attended his wedding, in Shanghai, to a Russian widow who was a barmaid in Shanghai's "Pig and Whistle".

Vic Oliver often wondered later about a strange incident that occurred after the ceremony. An ancient Chinese soothsayer with a considerable reputation of being able "to tell one's future" was being good-naturedly chaffed by a small group of Naval men as he peered into their palms. Vic Oliver says the chaffing increased even more when he suddenly dropped the hand of Charles Goodyear and said not a word.

Could the old man have seen that there was so little future to foretell?

Many more of Judy's friends were to die in the terrible days which followed the fall of Singapore.

Rear-Admiral Spooner completed his plans for the departure of the remaining little ships. He insisted, because of the behaviour of the Japanese victors in Hong Kong, that priority should be given to Military Nursing Sisters, some key personnel of the Fighting Services, and as many women and children as possible, in that order.

On that fateful Friday, February 13th, 1942, the embarkation of passengers began—not, in every case, with complete success. Some of the very small boats—power launches and motor-boats—were commandeered by armed deserters after, in some cases, forcibly ejecting women and children.

On the *Grasshopper* and *Dragonfly*, however, the embarkation proceeded as smoothly as was humanly possible under the chaotic conditions that prevailed. The crew carried aboard frightened children; comforted bewildered women; turned back would-be stowaways.

On the *Grasshopper*, Judy was seemingly determined to personally welcome aboard every newcomer, her gently waving tail having apparently discovered the secret of perpetual motion. She seemed to sense the gravity of the situation and so extended the comforting muzzle of her moist nose where she could.

The children were her main concern. She walked around the ship with them, played with them, even slept among a group of them.

The British sailor, even in times of peace, is used to putting up with emergency situations but the addition of more than two hundred names to the *Grasshopper*'s sailing list stretched even the *Grasshopper* crew's ingenuity and powers of improvisation to the very limit.

Petty Officer White, as the Coxswain of the *Grasshopper* was responsible for the ship stores of water and provisions. He now had to provide food and drink for four times the usual number of mouths, and had also to provide all the extras which would be in demand—milk, chocolate, soap, toilet-paper, and the one thousand and one items on his long list of essentials.

George White was proud of the way everyone seemed to settle down despite the difficulties and lack of privacy in the overcrowded conditions—the Nursing Sisters were a great help and, of course, as nearly all the passengers were associated with the fighting services in some way or other they were used to disciplined organisation.

The *Grasshopper*'s Commanding Officer (Commander J. S. Hoffman, RN Ret.) and his First Lieutenant (Lieutenant D. R. Campbell, RN VR) were preparing to take the ship to sea. This entailed, among various other things, the examination of charts, the calculation of tides, the study of "Enemy Sighted" reports, and the close examination of "Swept Channel" reports—reports concerning the areas which had been swept clear of mines during each day.

They studied, too, the recently received reports on the sinking, that day, of the *Scorpion, Redang, Siang Wo* and *Giang Bee.*

At nine o'clock that evening the little ships, bound for Batavia (Java) began to leave Singapore, a burning Singapore that looked to Petty Officer White like a scene from Dante's Inferno.

On the nearby islands of Bukum and Sabarok, too, the oil and petrol tanks were going up in flames. The huge spreading palls of thick black smoke reflected the red glare of the flames far beneath.

It was, indeed, an inferno, with the devil's own orchestra producing deafening sound effects—the shattering exploding of bombs, the roar of defending guns, and the frightening scalp-prickling sound as from thousands of wailing banshees at a distant football ground. Occasionally the coastal searchlights would make a fast sweep into the blackened sky.

At dawn the *Grasshopper* was heading for the Berhala Strait in company with the *Dragonfly,* a dockyard tug, and two double-decker ex-pleasure steamers. The sea was flat calm, the sky was cloudless.

Away in the distance to port, from somewhere behind the cluster of small islands, came the sound of explosions and gunfire. The first casualties of the day—the first of many casualties of that terrible day—were already being bombed and sunk.

Three small ships travelling together—*Kuala, Kung Wo* and *Tien Kwang*—had anchored, that morning, close in to the island of Pombong, where they intended to remain —camouflaged—during the hours of daylight. Men had, in fact, already been landed on the island to gather materials for this purpose when the first bombers appeared.

There were few survivors of that merciless engagement of which historians have been unable to produce anything other than question-marks. We now know, however, that some survivors, after five days on the island, were able to reach Sinkep.

One of those survivors was Frank Williams, the young Royal Air Force technician who was to become the master Judy searched for.

The "Swept Channel" route extended southward from Singapore, via the Durian and Berhala Straits to the Banka Strait. Along this route the little ships steamed in their bid for freedom.

The *Shu Kwang* was the next to go. She had only cleared the Durian Strait when, alone and unarmed, she disappeared beneath a hail of bombs.

There were few, if any, survivors.

The *Li Wo* (Lieutenant T. Wilkinson, RNR) was exceptionally unlucky in that she approached the Banka Strait at exactly the same time as the Japanese Invasion Fleet bound for Sumatra, and she was sandwiched between two converging lines of enemy transport vessels, each line led by a cruiser and tailed by a destroyer.

Her one four-inch gun barking defiance at the enemy's concentrated fire, the *Li Wo* headed for the nearest enemy transport. She succeeded in inflicting considerable damage on two of the transport vessels before her gun was silenced.

As a final gesture of defiance, the little ship then rammed the nearest and largest enemy vessel. Ablaze and badly damaged, the *Li Wo* backed out of the gaping hole in the side of the enemy vessel then capsized and sank.

There were very few survivors from the *Li Wo*. Lieutenant Wilkinson was posthumously awarded the Victoria Cross.

Less than a mile away, to the north of the *Li Wo* action,

another loner, the *Vyner Brooke* (Lieutenant R. E. Burton, RNR) was making for Banka Strait. Caught out in the open, she received two direct bomb hits and sank. (See Appendix I, page 143.)

Before the merciful darkness of night came down to hide the many hundreds of floating sun-bonnets and Naval cap-ribbons, five more of the little ships were to die. And the last to go would be the *Grasshopper*.

# 7 Judy is a Heroine

WITH JUST a few hours of daylight remaining, Commander Hoffman decided to lead the tiny convoy of little ships towards the group of small islands north of Sinkep in the hope that the thick jungle on the islands would provide some sort of cover.

Judy appeared on the *Grasshopper*'s bridge and was about to be driven below when she pointed her nose to the north and commenced to bark—fiercely and defiantly.

Knowing what this meant the guns of *Grasshopper* and *Dragonfly* were made ready and opened up when the first enemy plane was sighted. The flat-calm sea, the clear blue sky, the nearby jungle-covered islands, the women and children crowded on all decks, somehow made everything seem unreal.

The bomb that hit the *Grasshopper* was real enough and the planes, seeing that the *Grasshopper* was burning, disappeared in the direction of Singapore.

The fire was soon under control. The two casualties received treatment : Commander Hoffman for a bad leg wound and Petty Officer White for injuries to the hand and arm.

Despite his wound, Commander Hoffman was still very much in command. He ordered that food be served out to everyone, and that supplies of food and water be placed in the boats in preparation for lowering.

Judy showed no outward signs of fear and appeared only to be concerned with comforting the women and children below decks. That's where she was when the yells of the look-outs—"Aircraft! Dead ahead!"—heralded the appearance of a large force of enemy bombers and fighters.

The guns of the *Dragonfly* and *Grasshopper* roared and barked as the bombers and fighters screamed down on the little ships.

The two double-decker pleasure boats stopped, both on fire.

The tug, hit by a bomb, disappeared.

A few minutes later, the *Dragonfly*, all guns silent, was slewing to starboard. Torn apart by three direct hits, she then capsized and sank. (See Appendix 2, page 144.)

On the *Grasshopper*, Commander Hoffman accepted the inevitable. Hit by bombs aft and amidships, the deck immediately above the after magazine burning furiously he knew the end of the *Grasshopper* was very near. He gave the order to abandon ship. (See Appendix 3, page 145.)

The boats and Carley floats dropped into the water and the officers and men of the *Grasshopper* set about the task of transferring everyone from ship to shore, a distance of less than a hundred yards—a hundred yards which, because of the continuous machine-gunning by enemy fighters, seemed to take hours to cover instead of minutes.

The wounded, and some of the women, were taken in the whaler. The remainder climbed on, or clung to, the Carley floats. Some swam the short distance to the beach. The bridge Lewis guns continued to fire until the evacuation was complete, then the gunners, too, made their dash for the island.

The survivors from the *Grasshopper*, although safely ashore, had too much to think about and nobody realised that Judy was not with them. Nobody knew that when the second bomb hit the *Grasshopper*, a row of seamen's lockers had toppled and somewhere beneath them lay Judy.

Many of the survivors were wounded, some seriously. Some were to die. With few personal possessions, little food, no visible source of fresh water, they were stranded in unknown jungle country with the knowledge that the whole of Malaya was by then almost certainly in Japanese hands.

But Commander Hoffman gave them little opportunity to stop and think. Strongly supported by the senior members of his own crew, he directed operations on the basis that the survivors were still his ship's company.

Among the survivors were a few Australian nurses, six Royal Marines who had already survived the sinkings of the *Repulse* and *Prince of Wales*; some women, one of whom was blind and constantly tended by her young daughter; a boy and a girl.

The remaining members of the *Grasshopper*'s crew cleared a small camp area just inside the edge of the jungle. The wounded were laid out on roughly-made stretchers and put in the care of the nurses. The dead were buried.

The Royal Marines were formed into scouting parties with orders to search for fresh water, while others were detailed to try to locate any local inhabitants or other survivors from the small ships.

Later in the day, when the scouting parties had returned, the acute seriousness of their position became clear. They were on an island—later to be identified as Posic—which appeared to be uninhabited. More seriously, there was no sign of fresh water and the lack of water was their most urgent problem.

Commander Hoffman then decided to turn to his own ship for help. He spoke to his Coxswain, Petty Officer White. "When the whaler returns"—it had been sent on a round-the-island voyage of exploration—"I want you to go aboard the *Grasshopper*. Take some hands with you and see what, if anything, can be salvaged. First priority must be water, medical stores, clothes and bedding."

Petty Officer White looked seawards to where the super-structure of the *Grasshopper* still showed above water. There was no knowing when the whaler would return. The tide was ebbing so that there was only fifty yards or so between the beach and the *Grasshopper*. On the beach lay the body of a dead shark that had been stranded by the receding water.

Petty Officer White did his best to ignore this.

"Permission to go now, sir. It's only a short swim, and I can knock up a raft on board, sir."

Commander Hoffman showed no surprise at his Coxswain's request. He would have been surprised if it had not been forthcoming.

"Very well, Coxs'n. As soon as you like."

Petty Officer White was by no means a foolhardy man. His many years in the Royal Navy had taught him to assess problems quickly and sensibly. It had also taught him, or so he had thought, never to volunteer. And as he stripped to his briefs he cursed to himself at the thought of what he was letting himself in for.

He ran into the water, struck out for the ship. He wished that he could switch off his thoughts. Did sharks always appear on the surface, or did they remain below until they snapped? A good swimmer, he probably broke the world record for the fifty yards dash.

Safely on board the *Grasshopper*, he set about construct-ing a raft from the bridge and wheelhouse platform grat-ings. He lashed them together, threw the raft into the water and secured it to the guardrail with a length of signal halliard.

Gently, he lowered himself through the small hatch to what had once been the officers' quarters. Still mostly above water, this part of the ship yielded treasures in plenty—bedding, clothing, pots and pans, cutlery, tinned foods—which were all pushed up through the hatch to be later placed on the raft. He found, too, an unbroken bottle of whisky.

"Medicinal purposes only," he murmured to himself as he climbed up through the hatch on to the forecastle deck.

He lowered himself through the open messdeck hatch, carefully descending the iron ladder. The water was up to his waist as he slowly edged his way in the semi-darkness. He felt there would be very little to salvage from here but he knew his search must be thorough.

It was then that he heard it—unhuman, part whine, part moan. The few hairs on the head of George White stood rigidly upright. He heard the same sound again, and recognised it.

Judy! He splashed through the water in the direction of the sound, his outstretched hands feeling along the bulkhead, then over crazily-tilted lockers until they touched first warm fur, then a cold nose.

It *was* Judy! He had found her—and alive!

Murmuring words of comfort and encouragement, he lifted the locker which held her, then cradling her in his arms he carried her to the deck above. He laid her carefully on the deck, not sure how badly injured she was.

Judy slowly got to her feet. George White watched in amazement as she shook herself, leaped to the right and left like a playful lamb, then sat down in front of him and licked his hand. Not knowing whether to laugh or cry, George White swore.

"You silly bitch," he said. "Why didn't you bark?" Then, happily, he yelled loudly across the water to the beach.

"Judy! I've found Judy!"

Much happier now, he loaded the raft, placed Judy on it then clambered aboard himself. It was an unwieldly craft and he was concentrating on propelling it towards the beach when Judy stood up, barked at the surrounding water, then jumped overboard. Swimming strongly, she circled the raft until it grounded on the beach Only then did she leave the water, bounding from one to another of her friends.

What was the reason for her strange behaviour in the

water? George White was convinced that Judy's radar system had sensed something there, and acted in the only way she could to safeguard her rescuer. Just as there had been a leopard in the bush at Journey's End, there was surely a shark in the water near Posic.

As the raft continued to bring the necessary items from the wreck of the *Grasshopper*, the search for fresh water went on.

The position was becoming critical so a Chief Petty Officer tried to enlist Judy's aid. Just when he thought that she understood what they were looking for, she'd lope back to the water's edge, there to wallow and splash in the shallow ebbing water. She whined, walked backwards until she was again on the beach, then barked.

One of the Royal Marines looked up from his task of building a cooking-range designed to cook or boil without producing the give-away volume of smoke which would come from an open fire.

"What's up with your dog, Chief? Can she see something out there that we can't?"

The Chief, calling comforting words, moved down the beach to where Judy still followed the receding tide. Kneeling beside her, he patted her head and shoulders.

"What's up then, old girl?"

Judy, whining excitedly, began to dig in the wet sand. Curious, the Chief joined in the digging stopping only when clearer water surged up from the bottom.

Water!

He scooped up some and tasted it. Fresh water!

The Chief stood up, yelled to the others.

"Water! Judy's found water!"

Later, when the frugal evening meal was being served, the Chief raised his mug of ship's cocoa, spoke aloud.

"To Judy."

At the mention of her name, Judy looked around, wagged her tail, then snuggled down between the two children, shut her eyes and went to sleep.

The finding of a source of fresh water resolved many of their immediate problems, but few of the survivors had any illusions about the gravity of the situation.

During the afternoon they were joined by the few survivors from the *Dragonfly*. Leading Stoker Les Searle reported to Commander Hoffman.

"We were hit by two bombs, sir and sank almost immediately. The wounded are still on the next island, sir, with ERA Williams in charge. No officer survived, sir. Lieutenant Shellard died on the island."

Whatever his thoughts, Commander Hoffman's face remained expressionless. He looked up from his apparent contemplation of his injured leg.

"Thank you, Searle. See my Coxs'n and have your chaps all moved over here with us. We'll have another talk later on."

One result of their talk that evening was the decision to send the *Dragonfly*'s whaler southwards to the island of Sinkep where they would try to obtain transport for the remainder. If this failed they would come back and use the whaler as a do-it-yourself ferry.

The whaler set off at dusk, and not long after it had left the daughter of the blind woman approached Petty Officer White with news of additional but urgent emergencies. Two of the women, both of Dutch nationality, who were both in an advanced state of pregnancy when they left Singapore, were about to give birth to their babies.

The camp site already looked like a front-line casualty station with the *Dragonfly*'s wounded being attended to as fast as the hard-pressed nurses and their helpers could get around to them. They wouldn't be able to help so Petty Officer White decided he would have to deliver the babies himself—after all, during the Spanish War had he not assisted at a birth on HMS *Grenville*?

With the blind woman's daughter at his side, before midnight he had brought two baby boys into the world, and the umbilical cords were cut with his bowie knife.

Two days later the babies were baptised in the sea and Petty Officer George Leonard White proudly puffed out like a pouter pigeon when he heard one christened George, the other Leonard.

For the next few days each man and woman fought a personal and never-ending battle against the huge ants and small sandlice, and against the many varieties of exploring spiders and lizards.

The island teemed with snakes of varied hues and size and Judy soon showed that she was a force to be reckoned with. She would leap around the venturesome snake, stiff-legged like a bucking bronco, until, seeing her chance, she would strike with paw and teeth until the reptile died. Head held high, she would then carry it to whoever was particularly favoured at that moment, deposit it at his or her feet then trot off to continue her search for anything else that moved.

On the fifth day after the bombing of the *Grasshopper* the survivors were taken off the island at Posic by a large tongkan and transported to Sinkep. After two days' rest they left their wounded in the care of the kindly Dutch Administrator at Dabo and again put to sea. They'd heard the rumour that at Padang, in Sumatra, British and Australian naval vessels were waiting to carry them to Colombo and freedom.

Judy, of course, went with them but Petty Office White remained behind with three others. These four men set out on one of the most incredible voyages in modern history—and because of this and their links with Judy, the story is included in this book. (Appendix 5, see page 148.)

# 8 *Escape to Prison*

JUDY WAS curled up beside them as the survivors of the
*Dragonfly* and *Grasshopper* set out in the large sailing junk
they had been given to get to Sumatra. The junk had a
crew so they only had to sit and enjoy what they expected
to be the last leg of their journey to freedom.

A small, closely-knit group had formed within the main
group—Les Searle, who had been promoted to Petty Officer
Stoker before the loss of the *Dragonfly* teamed up with the
three Engine Room Artificers, also of the *Dragonfly*—
Chief ERA Len Williams, ERA Arthur Baxter and ERA
George Chalcraft.

Loosely attached to that group were three other survivors from the *Dragonfly*, and each one of these men
played their part in the story of Judy.

Jock Devani was a typical product of the Glasgow
Gorbals : tough, rough, and afraid of nothing. An accomplished scrounger and seeker-out of unguarded eatables,
he could always be counted on to find something with
which to keep starvation at bay—and to share it out.

In all such activities he was ably supported by another
Jock, Jock Morton, and by a bewhiskered three-badged
Able Seaman "Stripey" Watson who had rejected, through
the years, all offers of promotion with the explanation that
"he wanted to remain free."

The passage to Sumatra from Sinkep was uneventful

but they all breathed more freely when the junk sailed into the mouth of the Indragiri River and then on up the narrowing river to Moelok.

When the Chinese Skipper informed them that the junk could go no further they began to realise that they would still need lots of determination—and, perhaps, a little luck —to reach their goal. Between them and Padang—where the ships were waiting—were two hundred miles of hot and humid jungle where the average rainfall was about sixty inches a year. In this entangled mass of trees and creepers lived tigers, elephants, tapirs, rhinos and orang-outangs, plus, of course, snakes, spiders and scorpions. The river mouths were infested with crocodiles.

Luck it seemed was with them and they found transport, in the form of smaller boats, to take them further up the river to Rengat. Yet another leg of their journey was accomplished in comparative ease.

What they didn't know at that time was that on the day after the fall of Singapore the Japanese had dropped para-troops at Pelambang and Japanese convoys of troop transport vessels had crossed from Banka Island to Sumatra. All strategic points in South Sumatra were by now in Japanese hands.

At Rengat, when the boats could go no further, the local people advised the survivors that they would have to travel the next 170 miles on foot, keeping near the river as far as Sawaluento where there was a railhead—perhaps they'd find there a train that would take them to Padang, their ultimate goal.

Spurred on by the knowledge of the ships waiting at Padang the survivors made stretchers for those of the party who, because of wounds or sickness, were unable to walk and with Judy leading the way, they determinedly set off along the beaten track beside the river.

The jungle scenery they had admired from the safety of a boat's deck suddenly became another thing altogether. Huge tree roots continually crossed their path and the lush

Her finest hour—Judy with her Dickin Medal, the animal V.C. With her (from left to right) are: Major the Viscount Tarbat, M.C., Mr. Clifford Steele of the P.D.S.A. and LAC Frank Williams.

*Photograph reproduced by kind permission of the P.D.S.A.*

Judy on board H.M.S. Gnat, 1937.

*Photograph : Bill Wilson*

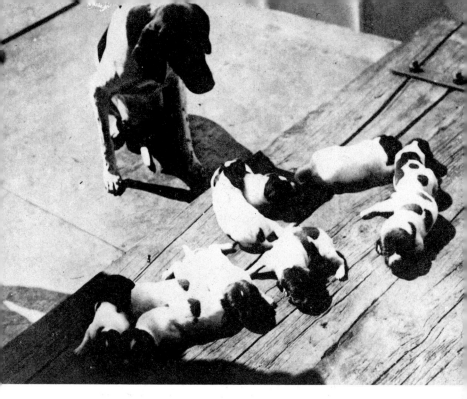

Judy watches over her first litter of pups.

H.M.S. Gnat, 1936—Judy's first home in the Royal Navy.

Judy's grave, Nachingwea, Tanzania, East Africa.

The plaque on Judy's monument, 1971.

IN MEMORY OF
**JUDY D.M. CANINE V.C.**
BREED ENGLISH POINTER
BORN SHANGHAI FEBRUARY 1936. DIED FEBRUARY 1950
WOUNDED 14TH FEBRUARY 1942

BOMBED AND SUNK H.M.S. GRASSHOPPER LINGGA ARCHIPELAGO 14TH FEBRUARY 1942

TORPEDOED S.S. VAN WARWICK, TANDJONG BALI MALACCA STRAITS 26TH JUNE 1943

JAPANESE PRISONER-OF-WAR 8IA PADANG GLOEGOER, DELI SUMATRA 17TH MARCH 1942 – 14TH AUGUST 1945

| CHINA | CEYLON | JAVA | ENGLAND | EGYPT |
| BURMA | SINGAPORE | MALAYA | SUMATRA | E. AFRICA |

THEY ALSO SERVED

green vegetation usually was just covering for the slimy mud which was the home of countless leeches.

Able Seaman Watson collected the first leech, on his groin. Startled, he watched the leech swell up until it was more than an inch across. He knew that if he tried to pull it off it would leave a wound which in the jungle could develop into a tropical ulcer. There was only one thing to do—apply a lighted cigarette. It worked and the leech fell off, taking only blood with it.

Judy, as always, seemed quite convinced that the whole party was in *her* care. She never faltered, loping ahead to warn of any hidden dangers. When she found the solid ground everyone, without hesitation, followed.

Then on the second day of the trek she began to bark at a lurking crocodile. Probably it would have been quite content to slip away into deeper water at their noisy approach but Judy couldn't leave well alone.

She was in charge and she meant all and sundry to know it. Barking furiously, she got too close—and nearly had her head bitten off. The animal's claws gashed her high on her shoulder and as she yelped and back-pedalled, the crocodile disappeared into the river.

Judy was too important to lose so the party, in concern, stopped at an abandoned warehouse to clean her wound. Jock Devani tended her gently but she seemed to have no idea how close she'd come to losing her life. As she was filled with energy, he left the others to rest and he and Judy set off to look around.

The party heard him shout with joy and saw the naval officer's cap he had "found" at Rengat go up in the air. Luck was still with them—they had unearthed a stock of Marmite. Determination was renewed and bodies restored as hot drinks were made and sipped with great pleasure; now they had concentrated food to last them a considerable time.

But that was to be their last piece of good luck. For five weeks they trekked through that humid jungle; their sweat-stained clothes were torn, and their legs were mud caked. Every day was slog and push on, slog and push on, but somehow they were still quite perky when, tired and hungry, they reached the railhead at Sawaluento.

Everyone at the rail head passed on the rumour that there were Japanese troops everywhere. No one as yet had actually seen any, but it was believed they were nearby. For the survivors, rumours meant nothing. Here was the train they needed to take them the last fifty miles to Padang, to the ship that would take them to freedom. Tired, but optimistic and cheerful they piled on board and relaxed as the train chuffed away.

The shout of : "There's the sea !" was wonderful. They had made it. Jungle, mud, wounds were all forgotten as almost before the engine grunted to a halt they were helping each other down from the trucks. Everyone was talking at once, asking the same questions. The answers dispersed their enthusiasm—they had missed the last ship by just twenty-four hours.

Now the Dutch officials had declared Padang an open city and anyone who tried to go near the few small boats would be shot. The Japanese were expected to arrive at any time and Padang would be surrendered to them.

The life seemed to go out of everybody. They were not exactly prisoners but the Dutch officials forbade them to leave Padang. For a whole day they haunted the docks, their eyes hopefully scanning the Indian Ocean, praying that there would be just one more ship.

Each step the Japanese troops made was passed on by rumour. They were getting closer; it was merely a matter of time before this last post was scooped into the Japanese net. And it was Judy who made them all aware that the moment had come.

She was lying in the centre of the small classroom in the Dutch School where they had been told to stay, her head resting on her forepaws, her eyes fixed on the open door.

Les Searle was looking at Judy, but he wasn't thinking about her. He was wondering why they hadn't made a firm stand against the orders of the Dutch Administrator while some of them still had their arms. They could then have taken the available boats, by force, if necessary, and to hell with him.

At the first sound of the motor-cycles, Judy slowly got to her feet. She stood tensely, perfectly still, then her lip curled upwards in a silent snarl. The seven men in the room knew, without a shadow of doubt, that the Japanese had arrived.

From outside came the sound of shouting, of harsh words of command. Les Searle slipped a piece of cloth through the collar that Judy was still wearing and pulled her protectively to his side as a Japanese Colonel, closely followed by three of his staff, strode into the room. A barked word of command brought the seven men instinctively to attention.

The Colonel, short, squat, his eyes hidden behind thick lenses, pointed to Judy, said something in Japanese, then turned abruptly on his heel and left.

Through that long night they sat and talked, always aware of the patrolling sentry posted at the school gates. They went over and over again the pointlessness of the struggle they had already had, showing their reaction to being taken prisoner in many different ways. Some were truculent, most were depressed; all were apprehensive of the immediate future. They talked of the rumours they had heard—that the Japs tortured women and children, that they couldn't be bothered keeping prisoners.

But the next morning it was obvious that they were to be prisoners of war. The Japanese isolated the women and children then took them away.

The men, not daring to even think about the women and children, were marshalled into four main groups— British, Dutch, Australian, and all officers—and were marched through the town to the Dutch army barracks.

Each group was housed in a separate block, another contained Japanese prison guards, the last was a storeroom.

Each block was entirely self-contained, each having its own cooks and cookhouse, its own "honcha"—the senior man of that block who was directly responsible to the Japanese for its cleanliness and routines—and its own internal organisation. And the first and foremost problem for him, as well as the rest, was to find sufficient food.

The cooks did their best with the food, mostly rice, that the Japanese issued, but the amount for each man never was enough.

For Judy this was probably the unhappiest and most difficult period of her life. Les Searle tried to explain to the Camp Commandant that Judy was an official member of the Royal Navy but that came to nothing. Except for an occasional swiftly-aimed kick which Judy easily avoided, she was mostly ignored.

Les Searle and Petty Officer "Punch" Puncheon did their best for her but as she wasn't entitled to an official food ration, she was forced to solve her own problems in her own way. She stalked and killed her own food—rats, snakes, lizards, birds—and became a first-class scrounger from the more affluent officers and the Dutch.

The thing that most threatened her survival was her value as a possible meal. The Japanese shot all dogs on sight, considering them a tasty addition to the stewpot.

Judy, though much changed from Gunboat days, still had her animal senses and especially her increasing sense of self-preservation. She was able to appear and disappear at will, she knew which Japanese guards were to be avoided, and which men she should team up with in the constant search for food. In fact, Judy's choice of companions was to prove most profitable.

Some men, inevitably, were better at bartering, or scheming, or stealing, than others, and the most successful organisation in the Padang prison camp at that time was undoubtedly the group made up of Les Searle, Jock Devani, Phil Philby, Watson—and Judy.

The Japanese had allowed native traders to set up market stalls one afternoon a week inside the barracks. These four men—and Judy—turned Market Day into "Operation Snatch" day. Success meant full bellies. Failure meant at the very least, violent beatings. This did not deter them. While Les Searle bartered and haggled, Jock helped himself to anything within reach. Judy stayed near Philby ready to pick up anything he "accidentally" dropped, then she'd scoop it up and carry it to the waiting Watson.

It was Philby who planned and carried out the most successful and most spectacular theft at the barracks. Using banana skins as bait, Philby coaxed one of the two goats that supplied milk to the Japanese Commandant as close as he could to a window of the block. With a noose made from old telephone wire he caught the goat and hoisted it up to the window. There was little sleep in the block that night but when they did sleep it was on full bellies. Next morning, when agitated guards searched buildings and compounds for the missing goat, no trace of it could be found—no hair, no hoof, no hide.

Compared with the camps which followed, Padang, even if the men didn't realise it at the time, was not bad at all. The men were short of food, but they hadn't—yet—started to die. Each block had its own open-air compound in which the men lounged, exercised, played games, or sat around in small groups talking, or playing cards.

The officers, in their block, lived well. They were paid considerably more than the men, whose ten cents per day didn't go very far. And most of them also had money of their own, and valuables, with which to barter for food, fruit, cigarettes, even cigars.

The Dutch, however, were the affluent members of Padang prison society. They had moved into the barracks, *their* barracks, almost voluntarily, taking with them, from their nearby homes, all the comforts they could carry—

food, beds, bedding, clothing, furniture, deckchairs, books, cigars, cigarettes, and anything else which they thought would alleviate the—temporary, as they thought—discomfort of their incarceration.

The Australians and the British were the camp paupers. A few of them still had some money, but they were loath to spend it except on vital necessities. Very few of them had any personal possessions.

The British prisoners, philosophical, cheerful, made the best of things, passing the time by playing never-ending games of football or cards. It took the Australians to jolt them out of their complacency.

One morning, the eyes of the whole camp were riveted by the sight in the Australian compound of a number of the prisoners lounging in deckchairs, each smoking a cigar, each with a pile of coloured magazines within reach.

Each day for the following week more deckchairs appeared, more cigars, more books and magazines. Then came tables, bottles of wine and wine-glasses and, finally, an armchair for the "honcha" of the Aussie block, Sergeant Stricchino.

Nobody watched more closely than the Japanese guards but they couldn't solve the mystery of the sudden affluence of the Australians.

They made one or two inspection raids on the Australian block but always during daylight hours when all hands were accounted for. It took them a long time to find out that in the Australian block there was a manhole which led into the local sewage tunnels and that these led to other manholes, outside the barracks which led upwards to nearby godowns and warehouses.

Each night, after the last muster, a small party of Australians dropped down in the labyrinth of sewers to return, hours later, with the spoils of their expedition. And they might have gone on forever if they hadn't let the cat out of the bag themselves.

One of their "finds" was a medical book written in

Dutch. An Aussie prisoner decided to ask one of the Dutch prisoners, a doctor, about it. It was the wrong doctor to choose—he immediately recognised the book as one from his own home. The manhole system was discovered and there were no more night excursions. But there were no repercussions and the Aussies were allowed to keep what they had.

Judy herself had been exploring at night and the men had to make a stand about it. They always closely watched her during the day because of the constant danger of her being shot. But at night, without their knowledge, she quietly got out of one of the open windows, slipped through a small gap beneath a wire-meshed gate and disappeared into the darkness to forage for food.

Discovery came about when she dropped from the window on to the snoring figure of Petty Officer Puncheon, nearly frightening him to death. The half-eaten chicken, dropped by the equally startled Judy, told its own tale. From that night Judy was tied while they slept. "Not," said Petty Officer Puncheon in explanation to the woebegone Judy, "as a punishment, but because we don't want you to be eaten."

The days, the weeks, the months slipped by. There was no reliable source of news of the outside world, or even of the "inside" world they'd been forced into. The strongest rumour was that they were to be moved : some said it was to Japan, others said it was to Singapore.

Then came the official announcement—half the total number of prisoners at Padang were to be transported to Balawan, a seaport in North Sumatra, and were to be ready to move on the following day. Les Searle, Jock Devani, Philby and Puncheon were all to be moved and they decided that Judy would be safer if she went with them.

Able Seaman Watson, that great-hearted irrepressible "three-badger" who wanted to be free, remained at Padang. He was later transported to Siam where he died.

Les Searle climbed into a lorry with George Chalcraft, Arthur Baxter and Len Williams and they helped pull aboard "Punch" Puncheon who was carrying Judy. They patted her reassuringly then covered her with some rice sacks until the lorry moved off.

Les Searle knew they were right to take Judy with them but he couldn't realise what the results would be. Somewhere along the long convoy line of lorries was a young Air Force Technician named Frank Williams who had followed a similar track to Padang as the survivors of the *Grasshopper* and *Dragonfly* had. First he'd travelled in a Malay tongkan, then a launch, a truck, and finally a plane to Padang. When he arrived the Japanese were already in charge. He too was going to Medan, just like Judy.

# 9 Judy Finds Her Master

FOR FOUR days the convoy travelled by road—Judy going into hiding when stops were made. At Balawan the men were put into a disused labour camp but two days later they were all moved to Gloergoer, a suburb of Medan, where they were housed in an old Dutch army barracks very similar to the one they had left at Padang.

They were still grouped together as British, Australian and Dutch, but were no longer segregated from each other. One communal kitchen produced twice a day the watery rice known as "pap", the thin leaf soup, or the mysterious mess known as "ongle-ongle".

For Judy, again, there was no official issue of food but capably she looked after herself, sneaking out of the camp from time to time to search for food. Such forays grew increasingly dangerous as all dogs in the area were hunted, shot and eaten.

Les Searle kept a close watch on her : "Inside the camp itself she moved around quite freely and openly, giving the Japanese or Korean guards a wide berth. She always loped with her eyes on the guard and her lip curled upwards in a silent snarl, and her obvious hatred put her life in constant danger from a rifle bullet.

"Despite the conditions in which we were living, humour, although sometimes cynical and often forced, was still there. To despair was to die.

"Judy retained her sense of humour; also her wonderful sense of occasion. She always knew what to do, and just when to do it to produce an effect. And this was clearly demonstrated on what I call 'The night of the big search'.

"Private Cousens of the 18th Division—Cousens of the cheerful grin and ever-ready wisecrack—had a very special job. He was the official boot-maker and repairer. Not for the prisoners, of course; we didn't have boots. We were, at that time, making simple wooden sandals which were held in place by a strip of whatever material could be found.

"Now, for some considerable time Cousins and I had talked about raiding the rice store in the Japanese officers' accommodation block.

"In his capacity as boot-maker, he visited the officers' quarters at least once a week, lugging along with him a large sack containing repaired boots, belts and other items of equipment. The visits were, in themselves, highly dangerous. Close contact with the Japs, the officers in particular, was something to be avoided.

"When Cousens told me that I was going to help him on delivery days and that we were going to steal some of the officers' store of rice, I nearly died of fright. But Cousens was very persuasive, and I was very hungry, so the following day found me, like a hypnotised zombie, helping him to carry his sack of repairs across the compound like, I thought, two flies voluntarily approaching a particularly menacing spider.

"Stealing the rice turned out to be remarkably easy but what we didn't foresee was a routine search of our block the very next day.

"As the Japanese guards moved systematically towards the rolled-up blanket in which the rice was hidden my prayer mat was working overtime.

"I think that animals have a built-in radar system which picks up all radiations of different sensations such as fear, happiness, panic, sorrow, as, in fact, postmen will probably confirm. Judy certainly sensed the fear and danger in that room, and she also knew what to do about it. She knew, as we all did, that the Japs—who would at any time be quite prepared to almost decapitate a prisoner with one swing of a shovel—had a deep fear, almost horror, of skeletons, graves, or any other evidence of death.

"It cannot, therefore, have just been coincidence that brought Judy charging into the room at that critical moment like a mad thing—her ears back, eyes glowing redly. In between her bared teeth was a gleaming human skull!

"As she tore about, clearing and avoiding all obstacles in her crazy dash, the Japs yelled at Judy and at each other. I expected any minute to hear a shot—but Judy was no fool. One more dash around the room—then she was gone.

"She had, however, accomplished what I am sure was her purpose. The Japs, their voices still at a high, alarmed pitch, left the building. The search was over."

Private Cousens used to sit beneath the canopy of a small lean-to shed, cutting the leather to make boots for the Japanese officers, and repairing the boots for the Japanese guards.

He was very fond of Judy, and she of him, and when her never-ending search for food became more and more difficult he risked his own neck by hacking off pieces of hide for her. It was tough—but not too tough for a starving dog to chew and digest.

When, later, Cousens was carried off to the medical huts, where he died, Judy would sometimes be seen lying still and silent near the deserted lean-to shed, her head down on her outstretched forepaws.

It was about this time that Judy met the young RAF Technician who was to play such a large part in her life.

Frank Williams was squatting on his haunches in a corner of his hut, the tin containing his meagre ration of boiled rice in his cupped hands.

He knew that to stay alive every scrap of food must be eaten, however unappetising it looked or smelled. Every prisoner received the same amount, so there was no need to share with anyone—what he had in the cup was his, just his. Each man must look after himself.

He became aware of someone watching him and he looked up into Judy's eyes. Her eyes remained fixed on his, as she walked slowly towards him and stopped.

He saw the thin body, the faint suggestion of movement in her tail, the brown unswerving eyes.

He poured some of the thick mess from the mug on to the palm of his hand, offered it to her. She didn't move but gave a short faint whine.

Had he rebuffed her then, this would, without any doubt, have been the end of the Judy story. But he didn't rebuff her. He knew—as would any boy, or those who were boys at heart—exactly what she was trying to say.

He put the tin on the ground, placed his free hand on her head, fondled her ears.

"Okay, okay. Make yourself at home."

Only then did she relax. She accepted the food from his hand, then stretched out at his feet.

Judy, at last, had found her master.

Their adoption of each other paid rich dividends to both, not only in love and companionship but in many material ways.

The intelligent Judy quickly developed a remarkable ability to understand any whispered instruction from her master, whether in play—as when they entertained the other prisoners with complicated games—or in earnest, when Judy would retrieve the fruit which, in place of flowers, was placed on Japanese graves.

As the months passed, and as the occupation of Sumatra by the Japanese made itself felt, the food situation deteriorated. Japanese currency was practically worthless. Fruit, eggs, chickens, and other sought-after extras to add to the prisoners' rice, were more difficult to obtain, and bartering with local natives, forbidden by the Japanese, became even more difficult.

As Les Searle said, "I, for one, shall never again believe that sex is the main urge; the motivating power; the driving force. Food without any doubt at all is the main target for man's arrows, which is doubtless why someone once gave the now immortal advice to women—'Feed the brute'.

"We—the prisoners—were marched off, each morning, to various outside work allocations. For a long time we were occupied in dismantling the Ford Works in Medan, after which we transported the plant and machinery to the docks at Balawan.

"Prisoners who worked—and prisoners who did not work were practically dead—were allowed a payment of ten cents a day and full rations of whatever food there was a day. Those who were only fit to do light work about the camp itself were put on half pay and half rations. Prisoners who were too ill to work received neither pay nor food, thus aggravating an already impossible situation in which the sick man, needing food to recover his health, was further weakened by starvation.

"Although bartering was punishable by death or by a severe beating—depending on the mood of the guards— it continued to flourish. Amazingly, I cannot recall any occasion when a prisoner was robbed or cheated in a barter deal by any of the outside natives. Promises were kept and deals carried out often without the buyer and seller setting eyes on each other.

"In the old Dutch barracks in which we lived, the showers and toilets were still in use. They were flushed through narrow gulleys which disappeared through the walls to the world outside, and it was through the holes in the wall that bartering deals were conducted. Our appointed look-out would, at the approach of our block-guard, call out 'red lamp' as a warning. Our guard soon caught on to the oft-repeated words, but in a way that we hardly expected. When approaching our block he would proudly call out 'red lamp' thus warning us of his approach !"

Judy did her best to make her contribution to the communal larder. She would re-enter the camp from one of her dangerous forays, evading the angry guards, and would not loosen her grip on the rat or snake until she could lay it at the feet of Frank Williams.

The forays were dangerous not only because of the ever present tigers but also because of the dog-loving natives— not dog-lovers as the English are. More in the way that the English are beef-lovers.

But then came the day that Judy brought back more than food from the jungle. She was pregnant! Everyone was dumbfounded. How *could* it have come about? As far as they knew all local dogs had been shot and eaten long ago. There were bets that she would give birth to a litter of tiger cubs or perhaps goats.

With Judy growing bigger and plumper, Frank Williams was hard pressed to find additional food. And he knew too, that as Judy's plumpness increased so did the possibility that she would be considered an even better addition to the stewpot.

He was determined to keep her alive and her pregnancy gave him a plan. After Judy produced her pups he would have her made an official prisoner-of-war.

A few nights later, Judy had her second litter. Nine pups were born, four being judged too weak to survive were passed to one of the men for "disposal".

The remaining five, even in those harsh times, grew fat and this was the time for Frank to put his plan into action.

He'd seen Judy often enough show her hatred for the brutal Japanese and Korean guards, but he knew that for some reason she just tolerated the Camp Commandant, Colonel Banno, although she wouldn't let him touch her. Sometimes he'd threaten her with his sword, Frank believed only for the sport of seeing her snarl right back at him. And Frank knew, too, that the Colonel had a local lady friend who, whenever she saw Judy, would call "Judy, come," and try to pat her.

So one evening when the Colonel was known to be drinking alone, Frank, with a lively puppy under one arm, knocked at the door of the Colonel's hut. Usually a prisoner who had the effrontery to approach a Japanese officer would be ordered immediate execution but the pup, Kish, was an instant success. The Colonel roared with laughter as the pup waddled across the table-top to lick his hand resting on the edge.

He was very pleased that the pup was being offered as a gift for his lady-friend, and Frank took the chance to request that Judy be made an official prisoner-of-war. Colonel Banno said he regretted having to refuse, much as he would like to help, but he would have difficulty in explaining to his own superiors how there suddenly was another number on the official list.

Frank had the trump to play—if the suffix A were added to his own number, Hachi-Ju-Itchi (Eighty-One, Medan) Judy could be given the number Eighty-One A and everyone would be happy.

Colonel Banno, happily rolling the pup over and over, surprisingly agreed. As he scrawled the official order on a sheet of paper, Frank held his breath. Kish, oblivious to the battle of wits raging, was making a splendid puddle only inches from the Colonel's elbow.

Almost before the Colonel had finished grunting his dismissal, Frank was speeding back to his own hut, the precious paper in his hands. Before morning, Judy was wearing her own tag, clearly marked "81A Medan".

Les Searle remembers how the four remaining pups— —Rokok, Sheikje, Blackie and Punch—were great morale boosters. A constant attraction to prisoners and guards alike, the news of their antics quickly spread, resulting in a message, via a Malay woman fruit-seller, from the Dutch Women's Prison Camp—"Please can we have one of your puppies?"

The men rarely mentioned the Women's Camp. They knew what life was like in their own prison camp. What other sort of hell was it for women?

Sheikje, according to Les Searle, was the most attractive of the four, and was the one chosen to be smuggled out. When the Malay fruit-seller again visited the huts, Sheikje was given a whiff of chloroform from the medical hut, placed in the bottom of the fruit basket and covered with fruit. The woman then carried the basket out of the compound on her head. With nothing to gain but everything to lose she strolled past the Korean guards and safely delivered Sheikje to the Women's Camp.

Because of the difficulty in feeding the pups as they grew bigger and stronger, and of looking after them as they grew more venturesome, Rokok, too, was later given away. He was passed out through a hole in the compound wall to be delivered to the Swiss Red Cross Official in Medan.

Punch survived, and was still in the camp when the prisoners returned to Singapore a year later.

Blackie—that bundle of warm black fur—was, one dark night, beaten to death by a drunken Korean guard.

Les Searle likened the guards to spoilt and sadistic children : "They would, for no apparent reason fly into sudden and hysterical rage, and vent their spleen and fury on the nearest unfortunate prisoner. They were really unpredictable.

"One day Jock Devani told me that a convoy of trucks had arrived, all loaded to capacity with Red Cross parcels, and although I couldn't believe it, it was true. They were the first we had ever seen. What was even more unbelievable was that the Japs were turning them all over to us, lock, stock and barrel, unopened.

"The camp prisoners' committee organised and supervised the share-out. Bulk food—flour, peas, beans, sugar, oats, dried eggs—were handed over to the kitchen staff. Some of the parcels were then put aside for delivery to the Women's Camp in Medan. The remainder were shared out equally between all prisoners irrespective of nationality.

"Every hut looked like a modern super-market. It looked as though Christmas Day, only two weeks away, had already arrived, and that Santa Claus had brought us his complete stock of goodies. We were surrounded by, buried in, tins of corned beef, stews, fruit, meats of all kinds, coffee, chocolate, cigarettes.

"Some decided to have their Christmas there and then. Others decided to make their bounty last over as long a period as possible, despite the temptation to wolf now, regret later. The guarding of the stock became obsessional and this led to the one and only quarrel Jock and I ever had.

"We returned to camp at the end of a long working day and Jock was vehement in his belief that someone had swiped one of his tins of corned beef. Glaring at my neat stack of tinned foods, and declaring his intention of counting them, he stretched upwards towards the makeshift shelf. When I tried to push him away, his false teeth dropped to the ground—right under my advancing foot. There was a loud crack as the denture broke in two.

"The corned beef argument forgotten in face of the new disaster that had befallen him, Jock cursed me soundly and at length, before making for the Australian hut where, it was boasted, they could fix anything.

"He returned, grinning broadly, with the denture back in place, held together by a strip of adhesive tape. In a spirit of forgiveness, Jock made some coffee. We drank each other's health.

"Jock gulped down the hot coffee—then held his throat and began to go purple in the face. He was nearly choked to death when the adhesive tape, soggy and no longer adhesive, went with the hot coffee down his throat.

"If there were any way of doing it he would have charged the Admiralty for a new set of dentures. After all they were lost on guard duty."

D

# 10 *Voyage to Death*

FROM THE very first day that Captain Nissi, the new Commandant, took over from Colonel Banno, it was obvious to the men that new trials were starting.

Early in the morning of his first day in command he ordered all prisoners to muster on the compound square—and when Captain Nissi said "all" he meant "all". Those who couldn't stand were supported by their comrades. Those who couldn't walk were carried. The stretcher cases —the sick and the dying—were laid out in one long row.

He stood in the centre watching the lines form, his cane impatiently smacking his high boots. Then he saw Frank Williams appear with Judy at his side.

Captain Nissi stood quite still, disbelieving his own eyes. A dog! Not only a dog, but a prisoner's dog! He walked slowly towards them and as he drew closer, Frank Williams watched him with a quaking heart. Judy stood still, her thin body trembling slightly and her lip curled in a silent snarl.

The prisoners and the guards stood silent, watchful.

Frank realised that the moment was critical. If the Commandant screamed an order it would have to be carried out otherwise there would be loss of "face".

Frank didn't wait for the order. Fumbling in his tattered shorts, he fished out the well-worn piece of paper carrying Colonel Banno's signature and held it out to the surprised

Captain. His staff swiftly gathered round him and chattering and gesticulating they examined the vital piece of paper.

Being an "official" prisoner-of-war was no real protection for anyone, let alone Judy, but that piece of paper appeared to work magic and Judy was no longer the subject of interest.

He concentrated instead on the prisoners who were made to work harder than ever before. Even the guards drove the men as though determined to fill the medical hut to capacity in record time.

The second day was even worse than the first and had the pressure kept up the camp would have run out of prisoners within the week.

Then, on the third day, came a reprieve. Assembled again on the compound square, the men heard Captain Nissi read out the new orders issued by his High Command : "All prisoners are to be shipped to Singapore forthwith."

Back in their huts, the men were almost jubilant at the good news. Singapore offered not only the possibility of more humane treatment but also news of the war in Europe; perhaps, even, letters from home. At the very least there would be some sort of contact with the outside world.

Les Searle wiped the perspiration from the face of one of the stretcher cases, and spoke comfortingly.

"Cheer up, pal. You'll soon be out of this," he said.

That evening the guards visited each hut telling the prisoners to be ready to move off at dawn. Frank was different—he received a visit from Captain Nissi himself. The Commandant wished to make one thing clear : Judy would not be going to Singapore.

She was to remain behind in the camp at Medan.

When Captain Nissi had departed Frank was shaken. He squatted on the ground in his corner of the hut with Judy sitting as usual between his knees.

The problem was a bloody tough one—but it was his

own personal one. He knew he would get co-operation from the other prisoners, but one could hardly expect them to risk their lives for a dog.

"Especially," said Frank, looking at Judy, "such a skinny, scruffy dog as you."

But he was determined. They would not be parted—Judy would go with him even though he knew that if she were discovered it could mean death for them both.

Frank and Judy got up very early that next morning. Judy—wise, obedient, long-suffering—was about to learn another trick. This time the reward was life.

The young RAF Technician had decided that the only possible way of getting Judy to the ship that was to take them to Singapore was to carry Judy in a sack at certain stages where the guards might see her. At other times he would have to depend on Judy's strict obedience and her understanding of his signals.

Judy had to learn how to get in and out of the sack as quickly as possible and for more than an hour she played the game with Frank. When this was as good as it could be, Frank then trained her to jump into the sack on his signal—the click of his fingers. After this they could only hope.

Soon after dawn when all prisoners were ordered to muster on the compound square, Frank tied Judy to a post in the big hut, testing to make sure that the slip-knot would slip under pressure. Then he ordered her to "stay" and she sat down, her eyes glued to Frank's back as he took his place in the ranks of prisoners. Now there were *two* long rows of stretcher cases.

Les Searle felt the tension among the men increase as the Japanese soldiers counted and recounted the prisoners, and inspected the packs and sacks which contained their few pitiful possessions. Frank had very little to take with him but as it was essential to his plan that he should be seen carrying a full sack he had pushed a blanket into it.

When the guards—and Captain Nissi—were satisfied

that all prisoners were accounted for, they gave the order
to move out of Medan camp.

More than seven hundred men obeyed the order. Some
were carried, some staggered, some walked. They did *not*
march.

There was no parallel with the similar situation so often
depicted in a German prison camp, when the prisoners,
newly shaven, fully clothed, marched out with heads erect,
whistling a popular tune or cracking jokes at the expense
of their German guards.

The prisoners of Medan did *not* march and they certainly had learnt by this time not to crack jokes at the expense of *their* guards.

Frank, lingering at the rear of the column, whistled to
Judy as soon as he was outside the gates but as they covered
the short distance to the railway sidings, he saw no sign of
her. Moving along the rows of men as they climbed into
the train, Frank suddenly spied her—two bright eyes and
a nose peeping out from beneath one of the wagons.

He knelt down and the men, aware of the risk they were
taking, formed a screen around him as he took the blanket
out of the sack and clicked his fingers. Judy bounded over
and into the sack and in almost one action Frank had
hoisted it on his shoulder.

When the train reached the dockside at Belawan, Frank
released her from the sack and again she disappeared beneath the train.

The prisoners were drawn up in ranks along the dock,
stretcher cases in front. They were counted; recounted.
Their packs and sacks were inspected. The guards patrolled
around and about.

No one seemed to move yet somehow the whisper sped
along Frank's rank—Judy was coming! Frank could see
her at the end of the column, crawling on her stomach, her
body and head flattened close to the ground.

Between the ranks of men she crawled—and the
prisoners ignored her. Not one looked down. Almost casu-

ally Frank removed the blanket, helped Judy into the sack and lifted her on to his shoulder. The heads hadn't turned but everyone had seen—everyone except the patrolling soldiers.

It was taking a long time to herd the seven hundred men up the gangway on to the ship that was to take them back to Singapore. Most of them had already been standing or lying in the sun for more than two hours.

The sun beat down fiercely. Frank Williams, weak but determined, stood there with the sack containing Judy over his shoulder.

The lanky Australian at his side took off his wide-brimmed hat and placed it on Frank's bare head.

"If I fall down, someone will pick me up," he said. "If *you* fall down, you've had it, you and your dawg."

As though sensing that something was afoot, Captain Nissi appeared, slowly scrutinising the ranks of suffering men. He stopped in front of Frank. He had seen Judy tied to the post at Medan. He had seen Frank's sack inspected earlier.

"Ino murrasini noka?"—"Dog not come?"

Frank, trying to look overcome with grief (and that was fairly easy with Judy's weight biting into his bony shoulder) dumbly shook his head, looked down at his feet.

Captain Nissi grinned, moved on.

The column of prisoners continued to move until it was Frank's turn to step on to the gangway.

They had made it!

The ship that was taking them to Singapore was the SS *Van Waerwijck*, an old and rusted ex-Dutch tramp steamer which had been salvaged from the bottom of TendjongPriok Harbour at Sourabaya by the Japanese, then renamed *Sibiach*.

The holds of the *Van Waerwijck* had been prepared for the accommodation of the mass of prisoners—tiers of bamboo racks had been built into the holds, forming pigeon-holes, or man-holes, of approximately sixty inches by eigh-

teen inches. The very sick, and those who were unable to
stand, were slotted into the racks as though they were
already dead and were being stored in a mortuary. The remainder scrambled down rope nets into the dark holds.
Most of the hatches were then battened down.

Frank Williams carefully lowered the sack containing
Judy into waiting arms below, tossed down the blanket,
then climbed down the net. He carried Judy to a remote
corner before releasing her from the confines of the sack.

Poor Judy! Hot, cramped, panting, her tongue lolling
out, she stretched out in the dark corner, eagerly lapping
up the water which Frank had carried with him from the
camp. That done they settled down to suffer the short sea
passage to Singapore.

Les Searle, in the forward hold of the *Van Waerwijck*,
tried, unsuccessfully, to stretch his cramped body on the
wooden rack.

It was the morning of June 26th, 1944. The sun was
already high in the sky and in the holds of the *Van Waerwijck* the heat, and the stench, was already overpowering.

When George Chalcraft appeared at the open hatch
and called : "Les! You're wanted up here," Les Searle
thankfully climbed the wooden racking, heaved himself
up through the hatch. On deck, he gratefully gulped in the
fresher air as he moved aft to assist George in the now envi-
able task of cleaning the Japanese lavatories.

He looked out across the flat-calm water then stood perfectly still. He felt unable to move, yet somehow he managed to yell a warning. It was too late. Two torpedoes were
already converging on the ship. (See Appendix 4, page 146.)

When they struck, the explosions sounded the death of
the *Van Waerwijck*. They also sounded the death knell of
more than five hundred of the seven hundred prisoners
crammed in the holds.

Searle and Chalcraft staggered to the nearest hatch.
Water was pouring into the hold on to the tangled mass
of torn metal, shattered racks and dying men. The two

men flung the pile of rope netting downwards into the darkness and as they did so the old ship heeled over frighteningly. They grabbed, heaved and pulled at the few men who were able to reach the open hatch then they, too, slid down the ship's side into the sea.

When the torpedoes struck, Judy was being snugly held between the knees of Frank Williams, screened from possible view from the hatch by three of Frank's friends— Corporal Oakley and Laurie Symes, also of the RAF, and Bob Soames of the RAC.

As they weren't in the immediate vicinity of the explosions, the three men were able to scramble through the thick cloud of murderous fumes and smoke to the square of light from the open hatch. Frank, however, thinking of Judy, doubted whether he could carry her through the tangled wreckage and the mass of struggling, shouting men.

His own peril forgotten, Frank removed the deadlight from the porthole near his head and lifted Judy up. Judy, trustful and compliant as usual, allowed him to ease her forelegs and head through.

She turned her head towards him as he spoke.

"Out you go, old girl. Swim for it."

One push and she was gone.

With the ship heeling, preparing to sink, Frank Williams climbed and pushed his way through the darkness with the incoming water well above his waist. He hauled himself up through the hatch into the bright sunlight, slid into the sea, struck out from the sinking ship.

When he could, he trod water and looked around but there was no sign of Judy.

Two hours later, he was helped aboard a Japanese tanker completely exhausted.

His body was emaciated, oil smeared and his eyes were barely visible in their hollow sockets. He leaned over the guardrail as the tanker steamed back towards Singapore, his eyes searching the water in a last vain look for Judy.

Unable to see her, even to produce the solace of tears, he allowed himself to be herded below.

Judy, however, was very much alive.

Les Searle, swimming towards the far-off tanker, saw her. She was paddling strongly, her head held high above the water. He could see a man swimming at her side, one arm flung across Judy's back.

Searle swore to himself. Why didn't the poor bitch shake him off, save herself. She'd be drowned.

Four other men had every good reason to remember seeing her, as, urged on by strident voices from one of the scouring tongkans, Judy willingly turned away from safety to assist yet another exhausted swimmer.

Poor Judy. When friendly hands lifted her gently from the water she was more dead than alive. But there was no time to treat her as the heroine she was. She had to be hidden from the ever-present threat of angry execution— under a cloth which had been thrown over the bodies of two Koreans—and to remain there until the tongkan reached Singapore.

The survivors were met at the docks by a small force of Japanese soldiers who were to muster and marshal the prisoners on to trucks which would then transport them to River Valley Camp.

Judy was being lifted into one of the trucks by Les Searle, when all movement was stilled by a sudden scream of rage. Captain Nissi had seen her!

At his screamed command, the meaning of which was sickeningly clear, two Japanese soldiers, their rifles cocked, stepped towards Judy—a Judy who was far removed from the gentle pet of Gunboat days. Her gaunt body was now covered in oil and filth, her lips drawn back from yellow teeth in a silent snarl, her red-rimmed eyes burning their hatred of the man screaming in front of her.

Then a louder and more authoritative voice was heard. Colonel Banno, the Camp Commandant who had signed the paper making Judy an official prisoner-of-war, had also come to the docks to meet survivors. While he made it quite clear to Captain Nissi that Judy was not to be harmed, Les Searle wasted no time—he heaved Judy into the truck, climbed aboard and rapped on the driving cab. They were off—back to the prison compound, and for the time being at least, comparative safety.

When Frank Williams arrived at the compound he was, as Jock Devani would have said, "heading for the end hut". Weak, mentally and physically exhausted by the events of the past twenty-four hours, he seemed to be losing his fierce determination to survive.

Painfully he climbed down from the truck and started blindly to follow the group of walking skeletons to their designated hut. So defeated was he that he could feel neither protest nor resentment when a heavy blow from behind sent him sprawling face downward, in the dirt.

At first he thought he had incurred a soldier's wrath then unmoving, unbelieving, he heard the low whine, felt the cold muzzle and scrabbling paws. It was Judy! She flung herself upon him in a frenzy of wild joy.

He rolled on to his back; grabbed her; hugged her. No words were necessary. He felt that his heart would break as he looked into her tired, subdued eyes, as he felt the crusted dirt on her body.

Judy was content to just lie there sprawled across her beloved master, to feel his comforting, reassuring arms around her.

On her arrival at the camp she had refused to accompany Les Searle into his hut. Instead she had gone into every hut searching for Frank. She had circled and quartered the whole area of the camp, and, not finding him, she had settled down to watch and wait just inside the prison camp gate, her nose pressed to her outstretched forepaws, her sad eyes fixed on the influx of newcomers. Her wait had been rewarded.

Frank got to his feet, picked Judy up in his arms.

"Come on old girl," he said, "and stop acting so daft."

It looked, from a distance, very much as though Frank Williams was crying but at least, by the bearing of his shoulders, his determination to survive was restored.

Singapore proved to be little or no improvement on Medan. There was no mail. There was very little news, and there was certainly no more food—not for the prisoners, anyhow.

From what could be seen from the camp windows and from the open lorries which carried the prisoner working parties to the docks, the city after more than two years of Japanese occupation, was very much as it used to be, especially after dark when the neon signs blazed and flickered, and music from the many night clubs punctured the warm night air.

Then four weeks after the sinking of the *Van Waerwijck* the men from Medan were told that they were to return to Sumatra. This time, said the Camp Commandant, on a very special mission. It was something to do, he said, with producing cereal and fruit crops. And only the lucky ones passed as medically fit would be allowed to go.

The fitness test was farcical. The prisoners were drawn up, in lines, at one end of the compound. Ten at a time, in line, they marched forward and those who reached the far end without falling down were declared to be physically fit. They were transported in open lorries to the docks then on to old paddle steamers which were waiting to carry them across the strait to Sumatra.

All the signs pointed to one hell of a "special mission" awaiting them in Sumatra. Even the comparative ease with which Frank Williams smuggled Judy aboard the steamer made one wonder if, perhaps, they were destined never to return.

The crossing, to the mouth of the Srak-Sri-Indrapura river was uneventful. They were not, apparently, to return to Medan.

They were, in fact, making for Sawaluento in central Sumatra—and they were doing it the hard way. A forced march through the jungle gave them a foretaste of things to come, and their arrival, at night in torrential rain, rammed home to the few remaining optimists just what they were in for. Wet, cold, exhausted, unfed, the prisoners were herded into a collection of broken-down huts to await the dawn.

Judy was still with them—only because of Frank. Young, frail, equally as exhausted as the others, somehow he had found the strength, born of determination, to carry the dog over the more difficult parts of their forced march across Sumatra—across raging streams, dangerous swamps and crazy bridges.

During that first night of their new and secret mission she lay stretched out at Frank's feet. Tired, aching, hungry, but ever-watchful, her eyes would open at each sound in the night until, reassured, she would move her thin body slightly as though to make sure that Frank was still there. Only then did she lower her muzzle on to her forepaws and close her tired eyes.

# I I  *Hell's Railway*

"They would stagger to their work place
Though they really ought to die,
And would mutter in their beards
'If that bitch can, so can I.' "*

LONG BEFORE the start of the war, the Dutch in Sumatra
had planned to connect Pakan Baru and Palembang by
railway, a distance of more than 300 miles. The engineers,
after surveying the proposed route, then decided that the
project would be much too difficult and too costly. But
what they found to be impracticable, the Japanese deemed
not only possible, but necessary. And they had the advantage of an unlimited source of labour in the thousands
of prisoners and natives already on hand.

Les Searle believed that the return to Sumatra signalled
that the men had finally reached the very bottom of
degradation.

"We were used as a railway construction gang; slave
labour of the lowest, and cheapest, kind. We were expend-
able—lost men in a lost world—and living was reduced to
the basic simplicity of work and sleep.

"We had long since accepted that our chances of survival were, at best, very slim, and that our daily round

* From a poem written by an unknown prisoner at Medan.

would include not only unceasing toil from dawn to dusk but humiliation upon humiliation, starvation and disease.

"Worst of all, I think, was the feeling that we were, as far as the rest of the world was concerned, already dead. We received no mail, no news, no word, except from the ever-yelling Japs—and the few 'official' postcards that were at one time issued to us travelled no further than the nearest Japanese cooking fire.

"Every morning, first light brought the screamed commands of the guards—'Kura! Kura!' I never did know what the words really meant, but the implication was usually clear enough. It was always something they wanted done and it was most unfortunate for the luckless prisoner who failed to understand just what was required of him. But what a stupid way to die—to be beaten to death with a shovel just because one did not understand Japanése.

"When we first started to work on the railway I was rather lucky in that I was one of a work force of thirty prisoners who under the guard and supervision of twelve Japs—two of whom were 'engineeros'—worked ahead of the steadily advancing railway.

"Our job was to ensure a continuation of advance camp sites. In virgin jungle country miles ahead of the railhead, the Jap engineers would choose a suitable site—always, if possible, near a stream. We would then clear the area of trees and bush, and erect the group of huts which would accommodate the railway construction gangs when the railhead had sufficiently advanced.

"The work progressed with all the speed and precision of a modern factory. We cleared the site, split bamboos battering ram fashion, against an axe-head lashed to a tree. Ropes were made from fibrous vines, roofs were thatched with leaves, rain ditches and latrines were dug. In that jungle we toiled and sweated from dawn till dusk. Any hope we had of survival started to fade after a few months when I joined up with the main group of prisoners on the railway itself.

"The scene was one of unbelievable horror. Hour after endless hour, dreadful skeleton-like figures shovelled, heaved, slaved and groaned. This, I thought, must be the very nadir of man's inhumanity to man.

"There were no medical supplies. Every prisoner had tropical skin ulcers, some as big as saucers. Men were dying from beri-beri, malaria, cerebral malaria, heat and exhaustion, starvation. At one time, they died at the rate of ten a day, and every time the railway moved forward the daily toll mounted.

"But few died from the will-sapping effects of misery and despair—although they had every reason to. We grimly joked and encouraged each other and somehow we hung on to the slender thread of life."

The principles of railway construction as advanced by the Japanese were simple, often ingenious and very direct. There were three groups involved. The first went ahead to set up camp, the second built the railway embankment on which the rails were to be laid and the third laid the rails and sleepers. This was undoubtedly the hardest working group of them all, and one that took the biggest toll of men.

And behind them, always close, was the engine, creeping along even as the nails went down, pulling a line of trucks on which were laden more and more sleepers, more and more rails, more and more metal spikes which the men would drive with sledge hammers into the sleepers.

Frank Williams was one of those men.

Tom "Geordie" Scott was about the same height as Frank and the two of them became middle-men : "There were eight men to a rail and we had to carry it on our shoulders to the newly laid sleepers.

"We were at the centre taking the sag of the rail at its middle. Frank or I called the timing for our feet—left, right, left, right. If we didn't move in unison our bruised and bony shoulders would be going upwards when the rough steel rail was whipping down.

"Having dropped the rail on to the sleepers, we would then walk back to the railhead for the next one. The further the distance from the railhead, the greater agony to our sore shoulders, but the longer respite in the walk back.

"Judy liked to lope along beside us or just a little way ahead, sniffing and snuffling at the undergrowth. She was the one who put us in touch with bartering.

"If she stood still, her nose inside the thick bush, her tail gently waving, we knew that a local native was waiting to attract the attention of a prisoner with whom to barter—if he had the means.

"One of my most cherished possessions was a gold ring which, alas, had worn through and had finally broken. Its usefulness, however, had not ended. One day when Judy indicated the position of a waiting native, I bargained in whispers each time I passed the spot, covering the basic points of the proposed deal—'what' and 'how much'.

"Then when there weren't any guards looking I stepped into the cover of the thick jungle and handed over the ring. When I reappeared only seconds later I was a comparatively rich man—by prisoners' standards, that is— and only for the time being. The tobacco and coffee I had bought with the ring would allow me to barter with other prisoners, and I also had a few eggs and bananas to take back to camp to share with my own friend and partner, 'Dave' Davidson."

But it wasn't only in bartering that Judy was valuable. The men would watch her hop, lunge and snap in the bush and they knew she had found a snake or rat which she would lay at Frank's feet as her own contribution to the stewpot.

Even the guards appreciated her. When they heard her wild barking they would come running, rifles at the ready. The barking meant she had found something too big for her to handle and in that area of the jungle there were elephants, tigers, wild bears and pigs—all much appreciated by people who had little to eat.

To Tom Scott, Judy always appeared to have much more than dog sense.

"She was very quick to notice anything, to weigh up the pros and cons of any situation, and to act accordingly. And it was in a very personal and dramatic way that I discovered this ability of hers.

"Needing to urinate, I did it right where I was standing, on the railway track, and was seen to do so by a particularly brutal guard, a black-bearded Korean generally known as the Black Corporal although other words were often substituted for the latter word.

"Holding his rifle in one hand, waving a bamboo rod in the other, his face convulsed with rage, he charged towards where I stood, petrified, unable to move. He went past me, straight to the 'honcho', the British NCO who had been made responsible for the work output and behaviour of our particular group. He was a Royal Air Force sergeant and he was expected to bear, not only his own particular crosses, but also the crosses of his comrades.

"From the screams of rage that accompanied the wild blows on the sergeant's head and body it appeared that I had desecrated and insulted the Japanese Armed Forces, and His Imperial Majesty, the Mikado, the Emperor himself.

"He then demanded that the sergeant should, in his turn, beat me.

"Still being beaten over the head with the bamboo rod, the sergeant made a few half-hearted swipes at me. It was apparent that, at this rate, the sergeant was in danger of being beaten to death and that something had to be done about it—and quickly. Stepping closer to the dazed sergeant I yelled, 'Hit me, Sarge! For Christ sake, hit me!' until he at last began to strike at me with his clenched fists.

"It was a dangerous state of affairs that might have

resulted in death—but for Judy. She suddenly dived into the nearest jungle and began to bark loudly and furiously. All the guards ran to the spot, and the sergeant and I, putting our faith in the old adage 'out of sight out of mind', moved further along the railway to lick our wounds and hope that all would be forgotten if not forgiven.

"Of course, there was nothing at the jungle's edge to account for Judy's sudden excitement, but the diversion certainly saved Sarge and me.

"I was always fascinated by the complete understanding which existed between Frank and Judy—they were truly an amazing team.

"Judy was no longer a dog that anyone in his right mind would recommend as a suitable household pet. Thin, half-starved, always on the prowl, her eyes only softened when Frank touched her or spoke to her, or when she looked up at him. Whenever she found herself too close to one of the guards, her lip curled back in a snarl, and her eyes seemed to glow with almost a red glare.

"Sometimes this sort of thing would lead to trouble and when a guard threatened to retaliate, Frank would click his fingers and Judy would disappear into the nearby jungle. We didn't see her and we didn't hear her yet the moment he gave a low whistle she'd reappear at his side as though from nowhere."

Les Searle had a great respect for the Australian prisoners, working with them on that railway to hell.

"They were a tower of strength. Leathery, tough, stoical, they slogged on almost stubbornly, continually demonstrating to the Japanese that their spirit would never be broken. For this they probably collected more beatings than the rest of us put together. They were an example of courage."

Almost without exception they were big, tough and unflappable. Their work output was tremendous—not because of any fear of the Japanese, but because they seemed to be natural human dynamos. They encouraged their weaker comrades to hold on to life by example, and by as

much practical support as was possible under such conditions.

Imagine the surprise of the camp when one of the
Aussies known as Slinger volunteered to operate an ancient
steamroller with which the Japanese were hoping to pre-
pare a nearby landing strip. No one was going to say so
but it looked very much as though he was co-operating
with the enemy.

Slinger appeared not to notice the discontent and under
the admiring eyes of a suddenly benign guard, he enthusiastically set about the task of overhauling and reconditi-
oning the neglected roller. A few days later the scowling
prisoners watched from afar as the iron monster, with
Slinger at the controls, released a series of victorious
screeches from the steam hooter and rolled majestically
over the uneven ground.

He was seen surrounded by delighted chattering soldiers,
from the Camp Commandant down, and he spent the
remainder of the day teaching a Korean guard to control
and operate "Slinger's Sheila".

When he returned to the hut, Slinger looked around the
sullen faces of his mates then across the open ground at
the Korean guard who stood on the platform of the still-
panting steamroller.

"Okay," he drawled, "so you're all mad at me, but if
you keep your bloody mouths shut and your ears open for
ten minutes, you'll learn something."

In fact they only had to wait five minutes and when the
violent explosion occurred, all instinctively flattened on
the floor. Something fell on to the roof of the hut then
bounced down its sloping side to land with a dull thud
on the wooden step outside the hut door.

It was the flywheel of the steamroller. Of the steamroller itself there was no sign. The Korean guard had disappeared with it.

Slinger reached out for his food tin while the men stood
there trying to work out what had happened.

"I fixed it," he said. "I fixed it good and proper." And that's all he would say.

The few Americans in the camp had much in common with the Australians. Extroverts, enthusiastic optimists, they were adept at improvisation. One of them designed and built much of the equipment for the overworked medical huts—sort of Heath Robinson mechanisms, which were made up from the most unlikely collections of odds and ends. Nevertheless they worked.

Another American, although insisting that he had never heard of Buffalo Bill, boosted the camp's meagre food stock with some fancy shooting.

The men were working near a flooded stream when two bulls were seen on the opposite bank. The excited Korean guard raised his rifle, fired, and missed. He reloaded by pushing the bolt forward, fired—and missed again. The American, ignoring the possibility of being shot for his temerity, wrenched the rifle from the hands of the startled guard, dropped on to one knee and fired twice in rapid succession.

Both beasts dropped. The American thrust the rifle into the hands of the guard, then took charge of the whole operation. He yelled for a rope, tied it around his skinny waist, and plunged into the swollen river.

For some reason the Japanese didn't shoot down the bold American, and stood back until the two beasts were safely stowed in one of the wagons. And just as unpredictably they divided the fresh meat between the two kitchens—prisoners' and Japanese.

What makes a man voluntarily take on more trouble when he is already staggering beneath the weight of more trouble than any one man should be called on to bear? What motivated the American, "Buffalo Bill" and Slinger, the Australian, to carry out their mad impulses?

Perhaps Slinger, the big Australian, gave the answer.

"Heroes? We're *all* bloody heroes!"

# AT THE GOING DOWN OF THE SUN
by
Penry M. Rees M.A., 239 Battery, 77th HAA
Ex-POW Java and Sumatra

To the south of Pakan Baru
  where the nightly tiger prowls,
And the Simians greet the morning
  with their ululating howls,
Through the Kampong Katabulu
  and the district of Kuban
There runs a single railway track
  a monument to man.

In a short and fretful period
  that was eighteen months of hell,
Through the tangle of the tropics
  and the oozing swamps as well,
Through the cuttings that they hollowed
  and embankments that they built
They have laid a modern railway line
  on jungle trees and silt.

And in spite of tropic noonday
  and a host of wasting ills,
Ever southward went the railway
    to Muara and the hills.
Every sleeper claimed a body
  every rail a dozen more.
'Twas the hand of Fate that marked them
  as it tallied up the score.

Thirty times a score of prisoners
  fell asleep upon their back,
Thirty times a score of prisoners
  fell to sleep beside the track,
Thirty times a score of times
  the sum of one immortal man,
Thirty times a score of ciphers
  in the Councils of Japan.

On their ulcerated shoulders
  they transported rough-hewn wood,
With a dying desperation
  carried more than humans should,
On their suppurating feet
  with beri-beri swollen tight,
From the rising of the sun
  until the welcome fall of night.

From the rising of the sun
  until the setting of the same,
Theirs was just to grin and bear it
  and pretend it was a game;
Theirs was just to laugh and say
  they'd have a grill when it was done
And the cooling breath of ev'ning
  took the place of scorching sun

With the cooling breath of even
  came a leaven of repose,
And a narrow hard unyielding bed
  on which to rest their woes.
Just a width of rotten bedboard
  for a shrunken, rotten frame,
Where the bliss of sweet oblivion
  might eradicate the shame.

Yet the bliss of sleep's oblivion
  tarried long upon its way
While the bedbugs left their havens
  for a drying, dying prey,
And the ants and the mosquitoes
  and the scorpions and the lice
Joined the rats and noisy chikchaks
  and the jungle's lesser mice.

So another day was over
  and another day was done,
So another day of misery
  was all too soon begun,
But the mighty Tenno Haika
  and the power of Japan
Can't recall a day that's done with
  —and Thank God there's no one can!

"Show a leg, my sleeping hearties!
  Oh, get up and rise and shine!
For the sky is blue and cloudless"—
  and they feared it would be fine.
There was breakfast for the hungry
  if their stomachs weren't too sour
Made of boiling swampy water
  and of tapioca flour.

Back in England, paperhangers
  would refuse to use the mess,
But Japan must give them something
  and it couldn't give them less.
So they thought of those who loved them
  and with far, unseeing eyes
They consumed their mess of pottage,
  and the maggots and the flies.

There was someone trusting somewhere
    that a husband would return,
There were sweethearts praying softly
    there were candle lights aburn.
There was God up in His Heaven
    and he knew about it all,
And He heard their falt'ring whispers
    and He listened to their call.

And they drew new strength from somewhere
    and they battled for their life,
Though the odds were overweighted
    in this too-unequal strife;
But they kept on carrying sleepers
    and they struggled with the rail,
And they still persisted hopeful
    when it seemed of no avail.

It was "Kura!" and "Canero!"—
    if you straighten up you shirk,
And the one excuse for living
    is a finished job of work.
'Twas the mercy of the Emperor
    that saved them from the gun,
There was nothing now to save them
    from the task they had begun.

There was nothing then to save them
    from the toiling and the sweat
But the saving grace of illness
    that was more exacting yet.
So they welcomed their malaria
    with its vomit and its ache
So they welcomed their malaria
    for its semi-torpor's sake.

There was dysentery, pellagra,
 and a host of sister ills,
Beri-beri and Bush Typhus,
 but no medicines or pills.
There was every cause for dying
 and but few for hanging on
When so many fell asleep and
 followed comrades who had gone.

It was tie them in a hurry
 in an old discarded sack,
With a plank of rough-cut timber
 to support them in the back.
It was lower them as gently
 as a withered muscle may,
And commend them to their Maker
 and remain a while to pray.

But for those they left behind them
 there were brutish things to bear
At the hands of brutish beings
 who were only well aware
Of the primitive upsurging
 of an animal delight
That enjoyed the thrills of torture
 and the quiverings of fright.

They could drag their aching bodies
 to their grass and timber huts.
They could rub the salt of impotence
 in open weals and cuts.
They could steel their will to conquer,
 to forget, perhaps forgive,
But they found it mighty difficult
 to force themselves to live.

They had open huts of atap
  loosely tied to wooden poles,
And the roof and the partitions
  gaped and yawned in rotting holes.
Either side were filthy bedboards
  but a yard above the ground
With a floor of earth and water
  and with refuse all around.

And to rest their weary bodies,
  overworked and underfed,
Sixty centis of this planking
  was their homestead and their bed.
Sixty centis night and morning,
  sixty centis well or ill,
Sixty centis for each body
  and it had to fill the bill.

Many talked of playing cricket;
  many said they played the game,
But they let the devil rider
  take the honest and the lame.
There are many will be tongue-tied
  when the trump of doom shall burst
On the ears of waiting sleepers,
  on the blessed and the cursed.

On the twenty-ninth of April
  there was nothing to be done.
On the birthday of the Emperor
  they rose to greet the sun,
And his Clemency Imperial
  made a fatherly decree
That the slaves might send a postcard
  to their wives across the sea.

When the Day at last arrived
  and when the rest of them were free
They devised a Union Jack
  and they displayed it on a tree,
And they thanked the God that made them
  that He let them live again,
And they prayed they might be better
  for the suffering and pain.

There they left their friends behind them
  thirty times a score and more,
Left them sleeping in the shadows
  on a distant tropic shore,
And I pray that God Almighty,
  in the evening of their lives,
Will be gentle to their parents
  and their children and their wives.

Pakan Baru, Sumatra. 1944.

# 12 *Judy Barks a Welcome*

IN ALMOST every situation where people are repressed, a guerrilla movement will start. For the men in Sumatra, they could do just one thing—sabotage the railway they sweated from morning to night to build. In doing so they put their lives even further in jeopardy.

The sleeper gang—men who placed the wooden sleepers into position on the embankment—carefully laid sleepers on soft or pitted ground knowing that, at some time, the sleepers would slide sideways under the wheels of the jolting engine or wagons.

The spiking party, too, were effective. At a predetermined spot, they drove the spikes too hard so that they broke, or didn't drive them hard enough so that they would not hold.

And the men of both gangs did this in the full knowledge that they and the rest of the prisoners would have to travel in the wagons over the weak spots when they returned to their camp at the end of the day.

It was a grim satisfaction for the prisoners when the engine left the rails. They had slowed down the railway's advance but they were the ones who had to get the engine back on the rails again. But they did it time and time again without complaining.

In those long agonising months, these *were* special moments and any chance to celebrate was taken. When

Jock Devani—that tough buoyant character from the Gorbals—tried to convince everyone that the war was as good as over the men were ready to, wanted to, believe him. He was always the first to hear anything, and as he was usually very near the truth, there was a feeling of elation when he told them that the war in Europe was over, and that the Allies were everywhere victorious. "And," he added, "as a very special celebration I have brought some fruit."

He then produced a very large assortment of fruit and root vegetables which, he explained, he had found on a grave near the railhead. A Japanese soldier had been accidentally killed and when he was buried, his sorrowing comrades, in the tradition of their country, had piled a small mountain of gifts on the grave. As Jock said : "They would have disappeared by the morning, anyhow, and who more deserving than us?" And so it was divided out and each man in the hut tasted victory for just a short time.

Frank and Judy were in the same hut as Tom Scott : "Frank slept almost opposite, his feet towards me. Judy slept on the floor immediately beneath him.

"On each side of the central gangway, along the whole length of the hut, was a raised platform made of split bamboo. There were sixty prisoners to a hut, thirty on each side of the gangway, which meant that each prisoner had a space of twenty-one inches on which to lie, squat, or sit.

"Frank and Judy were never apart. Where Frank went, so went Judy. They lived for each other, and I dreaded to think what would have happened if either of them fell seriously ill. Both, I felt sure, would die. Had Frank contracted any of the many diseases which put so many men into the medical hut from which so few returned— dysentery, beri-beri, malaria, tropical ulcers—then Judy would undoubtedly have died.

"She would have been shot by the Korean or Japanese

guards, killed by the natives who hung around the peri-
meter of the camp in the hope of profitable barter with any
prisoner who still had something to sell. Had she run
wild, she would have been eaten by tigers or natives.
Without Frank, Judy would have died in any case—of a
broken heart.

"Not one of us was fit enough to crawl out of our
blankets, and certainly not fit enough to work for ten or
twelve hours a day on the railway.

"Judy was scraggy and bony. Frank was down to about
half his weight—just as we all were. They were both,
however, mentally strong and alert. They were both steel-
tough and courageous, and between them was a complete
understanding and an unbreakable bond of affection."

As the months passed, the prisoners began to feel that,
if they could but hang on, the end was really in sight. But
in each of them was the fear—rarely mentioned—that the
Japs would ensure that no one survived to tell the tale.

"Catcher"—a young gunner who appeared to have no
other name—was the last to suffer at their hands. Les
Searle was present when Catcher forgot to salute a Korean
guard : "The guard, screaming abuse, began to fiercely
smack the young gunner's face, and at that moment
Catcher's willpower broke. The astonished Korean fell
back before a hail of blows from Catcher's bony fists.

"His glory was short-lived because the other guards
came running to the Korean's aid. Catcher was roughly
manhandled and hauled away. When we mustered for
roll-call in the half-light of the next morning, Catcher
was confined, for all to see in a small bamboo cage in
which he would undoubtedly have died had it not been
for the success of Operation RAPWI."

Operation RAPWI (Recovery of Allied Prisoners of War
and Internees) was the overall plan but Operation Bird-
cage, part of it, was the one which applied to the men in
the Japanese POW camps. Set in motion by Admiral Lord
Louis Mountbatten as soon as Japanese delegates signed

preliminary surrender documents on August 28th, 1945, it entailed dropping hundreds of leaflets on known prison camps and Japanese troop concentrations. Printed in three languages—Japanese, British, and the local language—the leaflets gave notice of the Japanese surrender, and advised prisoners to remain in their camps until contacted.

Phase Two of the rescue plan then went into operation. Medical supplies, food, medical teams and wireless operators were parachuted into known camps, and the evacuation of prisoners commenced, by land, the sea and by air.

As soon as the operation began, Lady Mountbatten in her capacity as Superintendent, St. John Ambulance Brigade, began her tour of the prison camps.

Here is an extract from a report she made about part of the operation.

"On the whole things went extraordinarily well, and the recovery and repatriation of prisoners of war and civil internees was most successful and speedy, considering the gigantic areas over which they were spread and the endless problems involved, not the least of them the fact that in many places, for instance Sumatra, we had to do the whole of the evacuation of the prisoners of war before we had one single Allied soldier landed, or even the Navy lying off.

"There is no doubt that had the war gone on a few more weeks there would have been no prisoners of war in these areas left alive at all. They were absolutely at their last gasp, and the tragedy is that so many did die in the last weeks before the surrender, and even after.

"I went to a large number of camps where the death roll had been appallingly high, but the men who came through were in amazingly good spirits, however ill and emaciated they might be. This really applied to every single camp that I have seen, and the brave spirits and real 'guts' have been unbelievable during all these ghastly years.

"No praise can be too high for what the doctors, surgeons and RAMC Orderlies have done in the camps, even though they had absolutely no medical supplies, drugs or equipment. The way they improvised was quite staggering, extracting drugs from herbs and plants, making surgical and medical equipment out of old bits of tin, glass and bamboo, and setting up, in many camps, entire workshops which turned out quite usable stuff.

"The surprise of the prisoners of war at seeing, out of the blue, the first white woman for three and a half years, and she stepping out of a Jeep which most of them had never heard of, and certainly never seen, was truly amazing.

"I spent nearly a week in Sumatra, living in various buildings cheek by jowl with the heavily besworded and be-armed Japanese officers.

"We succeeded in doing all the evacuation of prisoners of war to the coasts where we got landing craft from Singapore to come and fetch them, and a large number also we evacuated by Dakota aircraft from hastily improvised airstrips."

In the Sumatra camp the men knew something was beginning to happen when Catcher was taken from his cage and stumbling, mumbling, was carried to the medical hut.

Tom "Geordie" Scott also recognised signs that the Japanese were accepting the possibility of defeat: "The beatings and abuse became less frequent and we were allowed greater freedom to forage for food. Some of the guards became almost friendly, and we began to believe that the end was really in sight.

"Then, one day, the rumour spread that the Japanese were on the retreat everywhere, and that the end of the war was very near. Dave—the man I'd gone through so much with—was obviously very sick, far too sick to work. Despite his protests, I insisted on taking him to the medical hut, promising to bring back something for his

supper and to collect him on my return. I went to work on
the railway and it was there we heard the wonderful news
that the war was nearly over.

"That night, when we returned to camp, I went straight
to the medical hut. Dave had died in the middle of the
day and had been buried that afternoon.

"Unbelieving, still holding the precious banana I had
managed to get for him, I walked over to his grave and
placed the banana on it. Poor old Dave—to go at that
time, just when the end was in sight."

With rescue and release only a few weeks away, Judy
came very close to losing her life yet again. For some
reason, she began to make her feelings towards the guards
even more apparent than usual. Her swerve from a Japanese kick changed to a daring, defiant stand and she would
crouch, only feet away from the offending boot, eyes glowing redly, big yellow teeth bared in a low rumbling snarl.
Only the sound of Frank's urgent whistle would draw her
away.

But being stubborn her defiance continued—almost to
the point of no return. It was a usual working day on the
railway when one of the Japanese guards started to beat
a prisoner over the head with a bamboo stave. The sight
was not uncommon, yet on this occasion, as the dazed
victim staggered backwards, into his place jumped an en-
raged, snarling Judy. The guard kept his eyes on Judy and
slowly lowered the stave to the ground, his hand curling
round the rifle which lay ever-ready at his feet.

Judy knew it was time to go and as her tail disappeared
into the nearby scrub the guard fired. No one heard a yelp
of pain; there was no canine cry, no howl, but when
Frank Williams called her to him further along the railway he found a raw streak on her shoulder where the
bullet had broken the skin. Again she had survived, and
had saved another prisoner from a severe beating.

In a world as austere as the one these men were in,
there was no way to reward the gallant dog. They needn't

E

have worried—Judy found her own reward just one day later. Frank, hearing her woofing and growling inside the jungle's edge, went to investigate. He couldn't believe his eyes—there she was trying to bury the biggest bone that either of them had ever seen. She paused when she saw him, grinned as only she could, then continued to dig around what must have been the remains of a long-dead elephant. Frank left her to it—if any dog deserved the biggest bone in the world, Judy did.

It was not long after this that Judy was officially condemned to death. And it came about because the Japanese discovered that the prisoners had lice. They were horrified—the prisoners could have huge skin ulcers, malaria, fever, anything, but they mustn't have lice. The only way to rid the camp of this insult to humanity, was to shave the heads and eyebrows of all prisoners. And to shoot Judy.

Frank Williams decided otherwise—and Judy became a ghost dog. It was uncanny the way she'd disappear whenever a guard was looking for her. Yet Frank only had to whistle softly or snap his fingers and she would appear. The game went on for just two days then it was the turn of the guards to disappear. Judy had come out of hiding and stood joyously barking her head off in the sunlight.

Judy, the silent one, was barking. Judy, who rarely made a sound inside the confines of the camp, was barking her head off.

In the huts the prisoners stirred fretfully as though in protest at being brought back to the awful realities of living.

But everything wasn't as they had known it to be.

Something was wrong. At least it was different. Although the sun was already high above the surrounding bush, there had been no bugle calls, no screams of "Kura" and "All mens out". Where were the Japanese and Korean guards?

An Australian slid from his place in the long row of

naked bodies, put his skinny legs to the ground, padded on bare feet into the sunshine.

Approaching him, accompanied by the still-barking Judy, were two uniformed figures wearing on their heads the red berets of the Parachute Regiment.

The promised day had come. The war at last, was really all over.

As the news spread through the huts, men staggered out to see for themselves. Some laughed, some cried, a few cheered. Many sat down where they stood, unbelieving, uncomprehending, sagging like deflated tyres after a too-long journey.

But for a few, the change was too much for their battered minds and bodies to accept. They just slipped away, quietly and almost willingly, into death.

During the night, the advance party of the relieving force had arrived at the camp. The Japanese, already warned by their own High Command not to offer any resistance, were taken away to be themselves imprisoned behind wire fences. Imprisoned not to prevent their escape but to ensure their own safety when the former prisoners began to fully realise that they were now free.

But that day the men were too excited, too busy, to dwell on the past. Planes were droning overhead, parachutes were floating down to earth bringing with them wonderful things.

The men looked on in rapt amazement as the food and equipment poured into the camp—meat, vegetables, soups, eggs, cheese, bread, biscuits, butter, jams, chocolate. Nothing had been forgotten. There were boots, clothes, cigarettes, books, pens, postcards.

While the kitchens began to issue real meals—huge appetising meals without rice—the medical officers set up a small hospital complete with beds, clean bedding, and life-saving drugs.

And, most important, there was rest for weary bodies. There was peace and the promise of a future.

During the next few days the camp buzzed with activity. There were frequent medical inspections, and informal chats with psychiatrists. Instructional classes were formed at which the men were brought up-to-date with the events of the outside world. Accumulated stacks of mail were distributed.

Then came the day when they received a *very* welcome visitor—Lady Mountbatten.

Compassionate, sympathetic, she moved slowly along the front ranks of scarred, sore-infested caricatures of men.

Only then did some of the men begin to fully realise that the war was really over and that there would be no more beatings, no more screaming, no more railway.

Some, for the first time in years, were crying.

Les Searle was there, Whitby was there, Judy was there, pressing her thin body against Frank's legs as though to make sure that he, too, was there.

Geordie Scott was there. He was thinking of his friend— Dave, who had been pipped at the post, who didn't quite make it.

Poor old Gatcher was there. Still only twenty-five years old, he was not yet showing signs of recovering from his spell in the cage. Blind to all that went on around him, he was holding, carefully cupped in both hands as though it were an injured bird, a bar of Nestle's chocolate, caressing the glossy wrapper, hugging it to himself. He didn't raise his eyes from it as Lady Mountbatten passed in front of him.

Impatient, unsettled, the men fretted away the days until it was their turn to be evacuated. All they wanted now was to get away—away from the camp, away from Sumatra, away from any reminder of their lost years.

Eventually it was Frank and Judy's turn to leave. Dressed in Japanese trousers and singlet, his feet in the almost forgotten comfort of socks and boots, Frank led Judy aboard the Tank Landing Craft that would take them to Singapore. There they stayed nearly a month in the hospital compound before receiving their embarkation papers. At last! There it was, in black and white—'To leave for England on board the troopship *Antenor*.'

Frank raised one eyebrow as he read the printed footnote. 'The following regulations will be strictly enforced. *No* dogs, birds, or pets of any kind to be taken on board.'

He looked down at Judy.

'No dogs allowed, old girl. Only ex-prisoners of war—and that, of course, means you.'

Judy looked up at him, gently waved her tail.

Frank continued to think aloud. 'If they think that after all we've been through together I'd leave you behind, they've got another think coming. We'll have to see about it, won't we?"

Les Searle, Tom Scott and George Chalcraft were amazed at how easily Judy got aboard the troopship without anyone in authority knowing. Frank waited until there was not much activity in the vicinity of the gangway, then he went aboard. Four of his friends wandered up casually to the gangway staff and started chatting with them.

Like a stage manager supervising the set off stage, Frank made sure the men were deep in conversation, then whistled to Judy whose nose was protruding from between two kitbags on the jetty not far from the bottom of the gangway.

A blurred phantom of brown and white streaked up the momentarily unattended gangway. Judy was aboard.

Three days later when the ship was well on its way to Britain her presence on the ship was disclosed and messages were sent to England requesting permission for Judy to land. Frank's relief was understood by all when he received a message from the father of Brian Cornford, one of Frank's friends, who was acting for Frank and Judy in England. Clearance had been arranged.

They were, it seemed, over the last hurdle.

# 13 *Year of the Dog*

EVERY YEAR is known to the Chinese by a name—a name which corresponds to one of the signs of the Zodiac.

The names of the years, in chronological order, with their Zodiac counterparts are:

1. Rat (Aries)
2. Ox (Taurus)
3. Tiger (Gemini)
4. Hare (Cancer)
5. Dragon (Leo)
6. Serpent (Virgo)
7. Horse (Libra)
8. Sheep (Scorpio)
9. Monkey (Sagittarius)
10. Cock (Capricorn)
11. Dog (Aquarius)
12. Boar (Pisces)

The cycle lasts twelve years and is then repeated.

It is interesting to note that 1941, the year in which the Japanese struck Pearl Harbour, was the "Year of the Serpent", and that the year of victory was the "Year of the Cock".

The year of 1946 was, without any doubt, Judy's year and, as one would expect, 1946 was the "Year of the Dog".

The voyage to England took six weeks—long restful weeks

in which Judy and the men learnt again how to relax, to enjoy each other's company without the pressure of survival and death always at their side.

When the ship docked at Liverpool, a fatter, sleeker Judy came down the gangplank, walking close to Frank Williams. Judy of Sussex was home—in a land she had never seen but where her pedigreed ancestors had pointed and retrieved valiantly at many a shoot.

It was a bad moment for Frank. After all they'd been through together he now really did have to say goodbye to the courageous dog who had become so much a part of his life. As the official of the Ministry of Agriculture moved forward to take Judy's lead, Frank handed it over with an aching heart. He had fought a lot in the last few years but he couldn't fight the law that required Judy to spend a period of six months in quarantine.

Judy who had had a certain amount of freedom even in the prison camps, was to be a prisoner once again, but this time she would have to bear it alone.

How could he explain to her that he was not deserting her? That he would visit her often at the Hackbridge Quarantine Kennels and that six months would soon pass?

There can be no doubt that Judy did suffer during the early part of the separation, but she was made of stern stuff. In the hands of the kindly, sympathetic staff of the Kennels, Judy did bear it, and the six months did pass, and Judy was again free.

Frank, looking fit and well in Royal Air Force uniform, collected a joyful bounding Judy on the morning of April 29th—a sleek, lovely Judy seemingly, during the first minutes of their wild reunion, all legs and tongue.

They were so pleased to see each other that the months were forgotten. They said goodbye to the kennel staff and left for London together—to a London which had already taken to its great heart the still-young airman and his now-famous dog.

They stood together side by side, before Major the

Viscount Tarbat who pinned to Frank's tunic the White Cross of Saint Giles, the highest honour awarded by the People's Dispensary for Sick Animals.

It was then Judy's turn. Reporters edged nearer and photographers' bulbs flashed as Judy was awarded the Dickin Medal—the PDSA Animal VC—and a citation which read : "For magnificent courage and endurance in Japanese prison camps thus helping to maintain morale among her fellow-prisoners and for saving many lives by her intelligence and watchfulness."

Frank and Judy really hit the headlines as this extract from the Daily Mirror of April 30th, 1946, shows :

### GUNBOAT JUDY SAVES LIVES—WINS MEDAL AND LIFE PENSION

She was wounded by the Japanese, saved the lives of British sailors, then shared their hardships in prison camps. So yesterday Judy got a "For Valour" medal and a life pension—from the Tailwaggers' Club.

She is a pedigree English pointer, and only came out of quarantine yesterday after a prisoner of war brought her home.

Judy was on board the Gunboat *Grasshopper* at the time of the fall of Singapore in 1942. Jap planes smashed the *Grasshopper* from which Judy was rescued the next day by the ship's coxswain. They were marooned on a small island for some days—and it was Judy who discovered a fresh-water spring, and so saved their lives.

They eventually escaped to Sumatra, but there they were captured by the Japs. Three years later, still a prisoner of war, Judy was condemned to be shot and eaten, but her execution was prevented by the guile of her master, LAC Frank Williams, and by the arrival of the British Liberating Forces, Judy was saved and later repatriated.

To Frank Williams the Tailwaggers' Club presented

a cheque so that Judy may spend the rest of her days in peace and comfort.

The next few weeks brought many more honours to Judy. Invited to the Headquarters of the Returned Prisoners of War Association in London, she was enrolled as the only dog member.

At Wembley, Judy was one of the four war dogs presented to the public as "Star Dogs of Blitz and Battlefront", and she appeared on the BBC "In Town Tonight" programme, during which she was heard to bark loudly when being introduced to the microphone. She was feted and petted wherever she appeared and was introduced to many famous people, including well-known stage and screen personalities, during her many fund-raising drives for the PDSA and the London Federation of Boys' Clubs.

It was quite evident that Judy enjoyed every moment, especially the visits to Children's Hospitals, but it was always noticeable that, except when with the children, Judy never strayed far from Frank's side.

Only when she could press her body against his legs as a reminder that he was still there, that he wouldn't leave her again, was she reassured. This pet of the gunboats, owned by all the men who had "thrown in" to buy her, had found her master a long way from the sea and nothing could part them now.

She was no longer recognisable as the scrawny often-snarling animal of the Japanese prison camps. Well-fed and well-groomed she paraded at rehabilitation centres at Sunnyhill Park, Ascot, and Gosford, wearing an embroidered coat bearing the Royal Air Force crest. She was now a mascot.

This pleasant interlude could not, however, continue indefinitely. Since the end of the hostilities, the strengths of the fighting services were being rapidly reduced and in July of 1946, at the RAF Technical Training Command at West Kirby, it was the turn of Frank Williams to be demobilised.

# 14 *The Last Post*

FRANK TOOK Judy home with him to Portsmouth, the naval port from which many years before her companions on the gunboats, Vic Oliver, Les Searle, Bill Wilson and George White had sailed. The next two years passed pleasantly but uneventfully. Wherever they went someone would point to Judy and say, "Look, that's the famous war dog." They were happy and carefree days. Frank walked her to his 'local', the "Stamshaw Hotel", where she would be the centre of interest. Frank would give her a drop of his beer in a saucer as her "tot". Most of the conversation was always about Judy.

But for Frank, the memories of the previous years were to be forgotten, not remembered, and he could rarely be coaxed to talk about the days in the prison camps.

He grew increasingly restless, then he applied for and obtained a position in East Africa with the Overseas Food Corporation.

John Hornly knew Judy from his days on the *Grass-hopper* before the war, but he lost complete contact with her until 1948. Then, one day : "I was going home on leave. I was going down on the escalator at Waterloo Station immediately behind a fellow who had a big dog in his arms. I recognised Judy straight away, but she was much fatter than when I knew her on the Gunboats. The chap who was carrying her told me about her prisoner-of-war days. He said that he was going to Africa to work on the 'Groundnut Scheme', and that he was taking Judy with him."

That turned out to be more difficult than "the chap who was carrying her" expected, as this extract from the *Evening Standard* dated March 20th, 1948, shows :

## A MAN AND HIS DOG

Young Frank Williams should be a happy man today. But he is sad.

Williams, preparing to leave on April 8th by air for East Africa to work on the groundnuts scheme, faces the prospect of parting from his dog Judy.

It was Judy who, after the fall of Singapore went with AC1 Williams into captivity for three and a half years. The Japs gave her a number—she was POW 81A Medan —and she was awarded the Dickin Medal for "courage and maintaining morale in prison camps and saving lives"

Judy, a sixty-one pound pedigree pointer, is not allowed to travel with Williams, and he fears that he will never see her again.

Man and dog have not been parted for six years, except for a period of quarantine when Judy was repatriated.

The major problem was obtaining permission for Judy to travel in the same planes as those which would carry him to Dar-es-Salaam via France, Egypt, the Sudan and Kenya. Frank was finding it more difficult to influence officialdom than he had ever found in outwitting the Japanese. But, determined to keep Judy at his side, he turned to Miss Dorothea St Hill-Bourne, the Secretary of the People's Dispensary for Sick Animals, for help—and immediately found it.

The overseas scheme was at that time under the control of Lever Bros., Limited. When Lord Leverhulme was approached on the matter, it was as though the problem had never been. Frank and Judy climbed aboard the plane at Blackbush Airport together. They were on their way to a new world and new adventures.

Frank Williams in recounting the story of their trip out, said that Judy was apparently asleep when the plane stopped at Wadi Haifa to refuel and didn't seem to notice the Egyptian quarantine official who came on board and proceded to spray the interior with a flit gun, explaining as he did so that it was merely a precaution against bringing disease into Egypt.

Frank burst out laughing, but watched as the official worked his way aft. Judy was suddenly awake but she sat still, watching and waiting. When the official reached her, he looked down at her—by this stage she'd closed her eyes again—then a slow grin spread over his face.

He pointed the gun. All hell broke loose.

The quiet drowsy siesta feeling of the plane evaporated as Judy shot up into a sitting position, her snarling lips exposing big teeth. By Egyptian standards she was a big dog, and at that moment to the startled eyes of the official she must have looked like The Hound of the Baskervilles.

He dropped his flit gun and made straight for the gangway. With the barking Judy in hot pursuit he must have set a record across the runway where he reached the safety of the airport buildings. When Frank whistled to Judy to come back, she almost strode on to the plane, a grin on her face worthy of any Cheshire cat. She settled down again to enjoy the flight.

Frank and Judy went first to the base camp in Kongwa, Tanganyika, and after a short spell here Frank was transferred to Nachingwea in the Southern Province.

Judy took immediately to her new life in this bush-clad area. According to Frank she was most enthusiastic about going on safari. This was a world she understood, a world where a reptile will attack, where danger comes in many forms. After Sumatra, the snakes were a pushover for her.

The men on the Gunboats who had spent many patient hours trying in vain to teach her to be the pointer she was supposed to be, would have been proud of her reaction when she saw her first herd of wild elephants.

Without hesitation she assumed a typical pointer pose, standing perfectly still with one paw raised, her head and tail in line. Frank leaned out of the cab of the Jeep and called : "Stop showing off. I can see them."

Judy really enjoyed life in East Africa. For her there were wonderful bonuses—like the time she went with Frank on a flight to Dar-es-Salaam. Frank was disconcerted because Judy had to travel in the confines of her own flight kennel. He was quite impressed when she didn't object and he was amazed at her contentment. Only after he released her on touch-down did he discover the reason for her contentment. Her kennel had an opening in the roof through which she could put her head, and as someone had piled a consignment of fresh game on top, she must have thought it was all for her.

When Frank found that Judy had devoured the central portions of the meat for as far as she could reach, leaving only a narrow outer ring of meat, he hurried her to the safety of the Jeep, trying unsuccessfully to look stern. For Judy it must have been as exciting as finding the elephant bone beside the railway. And she'd learnt the hard way that you don't let any opportunity pass where food is concerned—even if it does belong to someone else.

As the years had passed the bonds of affection and understanding between Frank and Judy had grown stronger and during this time at Nachingwea they seemed to draw even closer together.

Judy, her love of life never ebbing, was a first class guard dog, but even that activity had to have a touch of humour about it.

Late one evening Frank's house-boy, Abdul, dragged the tin bath in which Frank had bathed outside the hut so that it would be emptied in the morning. Everyone retired for

the night, then at about two o'clock Frank was awakened
by what seemed to be the sound of a huge vacuum cleaner.
Judy tore outside and began to bark furiously.

There, in the brilliant moonlight, Frank saw an elephant
sucking the bath dry with a wildly barking and cavorting
Judy rushing from head to tail, seemingly unable to decide
which end of the animal she should concentrate on.

Frank shouted and waved his arms, and the huge animal
lumbered off. Frank, satisfied that no damage had been
done, called to Judy and returned to the hut.

But Judy was not yet satisfied that honours were even.
She gripped a handle of the bath between her teeth and
despite Frank's protests, dragged the bath into the hut. She
then went outside, gave a loud bark of defiance and curled
up in the hut doorway.

Judy was never scared of any of the wild animals, not
even of the elephants and giraffes, and only baboons
drove her to a frenzy of annoyance and frustration. At first
it was a game chasing whole families of baboons but she
soon realised that there was little hope of ever getting near
them. They would jump around her, teasing her, so that
she didn't know which one to follow. When they started to
throw sticks or corn cobs at her she eventually decided to
retire from the unequal contest.

And so the days passed by. Judy had her third—and last
litter. The days were long and happy, a mixture of work
and pleasure. And the morning of February 1st, 1950,
seemed no different from any other.

There had been heavy rains in January and as some of
the creeks were reported to be running strongly, and a few
bridges had been washed away, Frank decided he wouldn't
go far afield for a day or two. But still he checked the Jeep
and as he did so Judy kept close to him.

Frank dropped to his knees and ruffled her ears as she
muzzled his hands. How grey Judy was becoming
now around the muzzle. There were even grey streaks on
her back and sides.

Judy kept her soft brown eyes fixed on his as he held her muzzle cupped in his hands. They had had four good years together away from war yet Judy needed constant reassurance of his affection.

He patted her head, rose to his feet, climbed into the Jeep.

As he turned on to the roadway, Frank gave his usual wave of the hand to those in the camp, then instinctively glanced at Judy. True to form, she gave a short farewell bark. She always did this just after he'd waved goodbye.

He drove towards a bush clearing camp, and with Judy curled up on the seat next to him, he had the chance to think of how wonderful she was, of their life together.

He could see her standing by the railway, ever alert to danger. He thought of Colonel Banno and the pup Kish, of the sinking of the *Van Waerwijck*; the proud and delighted Judy at Crufts, when the war was over and she'd been proclaimed a heroine.

When the Jeep reached the clearing Judy raised her head from her forepaws, looking up at him.

"We're here, old girl. Off you go."

Judy jumped down from the Jeep. Knowing that she would prowl here there and everywhere, but return to the Jeep when she was tired of it all, Frank made his way to the native foreman's hut.

Three hours later, when he returned to the Jeep, there was no sign of Judy. He whistled and called, but no Judy came streaking from the surrounding bush. For the first time in her life Judy had done something that had no explanation.

All the camp natives joined in the search of the immediate area. Frank, getting more worried as the hours passed, went with Abdullah who tracked Judy for nearly two miles along the narrow track leading to the Wagogo village of Chumbawalla. Abdullah pointed out the many signs of Judy's passing and, almost fearfully, indicated the leopard tracks which sometimes overlapped the dog's prints.

When there was no sign of her at the village, Frank sent runners to every village in the area, offering a reward of five hundred shillings for the finding of Judy.

But the days passed and there was no news of her. Sick at heart, Frank went on searching, calling, whistling. No one except him believed she would be seen again.

Then in the late afternoon on the fourth day after Judy's disappearance, Frank was surrounded by a group of natives all talking and gesticulating at once.

Abdullah was almost in tears : "This man come from Chumbawalla. Judy in Chumbawalla."

Judy had been found !—and alive !

Frank jumped back into the Jeep, called to Abdullah and the runner to get in.

Commonsense said wait until morning, for now the two streams would be raging torrents. Darkness was falling as well, but Frank couldn't wait. He wasn't even deterred when they found that the centre portion of the bridge which spanned the second of the two streams had been washed away. In such a situation you can only grit your teeth— and curse. The men hauled out the chain from the back of the Jeep then slowly winched the Jeep across the gap on a makeshift span of four tree trunks. After this, they sped over the last few miles to Chumbawalla.

The village head man led Frank to a low thatched hut. He opened the door—and there was Judy, alive but obviously in a bad way. She struggled to her feet, feebly wagged her tail, then collapsed in a whining heap. They wrapped her in blankets and Frank sat in the back of the Jeep, holding her close in his arms as they returned to Nachingwea. The faithful Abdullah who had driven back now helped Frank to see to Judy's immediate needs.

Carefully, painstakingly, they removed the hundreds of cattle ticks from her body then gave her a warm bath and dabbed her with disinfectant. Frank was satisfied when she ate a good meal then slept.

Each day with constant nursing she improved and Frank was beginning to think she was almost back to normal when, on the evening of the sixteenth, she began to cry.

Frank sat with her throughout that night. Judy's sleep was fitful and each time she woke she cried. By the morning Frank realised Judy was in pain and that she could not walk. He carried her, still crying, to the Nachingwea hospital. He couldn't reply to the many sympathetic enquiries along the way and at the hospital he somehow managed to control his voice sufficiently to ask for his old friend, Doctor Jenkins.

Doctor Jenkins examined the suffering dog and diagnosed a mammary tumour. He decided to operate immediately. It was successful and the tumour was removed. But within a few hours Judy was in great pain from a tetanus infection. She had fought all her life but not even she could fight this.

Doctor Jenkins was sympathetic but firm.

"Let me end it, Frank."

Frank nodded his head and turned away.

At five o'clock on that day, February 17th, 1950, Judy died.

Wrapped in the Royal Air Force jacket that she had so proudly worn at Crufts, Judy was placed in a box and buried in a clearing not far from Frank's hut in Nachingwea. The grave was then covered with large stones to prevent hyenas from disturbing it.

Frank Williams then began his last, and so definitely, service for his faithful companion of so many years.

Many, many long hours were spent in the African bush collecting pieces of white marble which were then laboriously broken into small pieces. The pieces were mixed with concrete which was poured into a reinforced form erected over Judy's grave.

When the form was removed, many more hours were spent shaping and polishing until the monument was completed to Frank's satisfaction. A monument, in Frank Williams' own words, "to a gallant old girl, a wonderful dog, which, with wagging tail, gave more affection and companionship than she ever received."

There was just one last homage to pay. Refusing all offers

of help, even from Abdullah, Frank Williams stood alone
with his memories of his dog and securely fixed to one side
of the monument a large metal plaque which read :

IN MEMORY OF
JUDY DM CANINE VC
BREED ENGLISH POINTER
BORN SHANGHAI FEBRUARY 1936, DIED
FEBRUARY 1950
WOUNDED 14th FEBRUARY 1942
BOMBED AND SUNK HMS GRASSHOPPER LINGGA
ARCHIPELAGO FEBRUARY 14th 1942. TORPEDOED
SS VAN WAERWIJCK MALACCA STRAIT JUNE 26th
1943.
JAPANESE PRISONER OF WAR MARCH 1942—
AUGUST 1945
CHINA CEYLON JAVA ENGLAND EGYPT
BURMA SINGAPORE MALAYA SUMATRA E. AFRICA
THEY ALSO SERVED

All around the world there are men who remember Judy
—men from the Gunboats who watched her grow from a
scraggy puppy to a sleek, fit animal; men who shared the
Japanese prisons with her and saw her reduced to a bundle
of bones covered in skin; men who worked on the Groundnut Scheme in East Africa and saw her in the happiest
years of her life.

Judy was a dog who inspired and encouraged, gave hope
and the will to live to the many caricatures of men who
refused to be beaten by "that bitch".

Judy will never be forgotten.

## Appendix 1 *(from page 66)*

The *Vyner Brooke* Survivors

THE FACTS concerning the fate of the survivors from the *Vyner Brooke* were recounted, under oath, before the Far Eastern International Tribunal which, after the war, tried and sentenced Japanese war criminals.

After the sinking of the *Vyner Brooke*, fifty-three survivors, including twenty Australian Nursing Sisters, managed to reach the beach on Banka Island, where they were immediately captured by a Japanese patrol. After being marched out of sight of the women, the men were bayoneted or shot, or both. The women were then forced to wade into the sea to be mowed down by machine-gun fire.

One man, Stoker Lloyd, and one woman, Australian Nursing Sister Vivien Bullwinkel, did not die. They dressed each other's wounds and cared for each other until they could make their way into the comparative safety of the prison camp on the island where they kept it secret that they were from the *Vyner Brooke*.

# Appendix 2 *(from page 68)*

Naval Historical Branch                    Official Report S7899

## HMS *Dragonfly*

At the outbreak of World War II, the *Dragonfly* was at Shanghai with the Yangtse Flotilla.

In January 1942 she had been engaged on patrols from Singapore and at the beginning of February had evacuated soldiers from Johore and had been shelled while alongside HMS *Laburnum*.

She left Singapore on the night of February 13th, 1942 in company with the *Grasshopper* by way of the Durian Strait. The majority of her passengers were civilians.

On February 14th she was attacked by Japanese dive-bombers and in the last attack received three direct hits. Minutes later she capsized and sank.

There were only a few survivors. These reached an island then later joined up with survivors from the *Grasshopper* and eventually made their way to Dabo, Sinkep, later proceeding to Sumatra.

# Appendix 3 (from page 68)

Naval Historical Branch                    Official Report S7900

## HMS Grasshopper

AT THE outbreak of World World II, the *Grasshopper* was the Below Barrier Guard Ship with the Yangtse Gunboat Flotilla.

She left Singapore for Batavia on February 13th 1942 in company with the *Dragonfly*. The *Grasshopper* and men and women civilians, Army and Royal Marine personnel, and Japanese prisoners on board.

Both vessels were dive-bombed on the 14th, and a fire was started on the *Grasshopper* but this was extinguished.

In the third and heaviest bombing attack several direct hits were sustained aft and amidships, and fires were started immediately above the magazine.

Orders were given to abandon ship and the *Grasshopper* was anchored about one hundred yards from one of the many islands in the immediate vicinity.

Survivors, joined by the few survivors from the *Dragonfly*, were able to reach Sinkep and, eventually, Sumatra.

## Appendix 4 (from page 99)

Copy of Letter from HMS *Dryad* (Royal Navy Navigation
School)

RE the sinking of the *Sibiach*. We are reasonably certain
that your theory (that she was sunk by the Japanese) is the
correct one. The negative evidence which supports this
claim is as follows:

> Royal Navy—there were no Royal Navy submarines
> on patrol in that area at that time. Three Dutch sub-
> marines (o.21, o.23, and o.24) were on patrol in the
> Malacca Strait and although o.23 (Lt. Cdr. A. M.
> Valkenburg, Royal Netherlands Navy) *did* carry
> out an attack on that day, it was *not* successful and
> cannot be related to the *Sibiach* as he could hardly have
> missed the fact that he had sunk three ships in a con-
> voy of four.
> US Navy—the US Navy have no record of such a sink-
> ing and this is supported by Royal Navy records which
> show that on that date the only US sinking was by USS
> *Jack* off Tokio.

From this, coupled with the reported air strikes on the
survivors, I think it is reasonable to deduce that the convoy was attacked by the Japanese themselves.

The Secretary to FOSM was kind enough to provide the details from RN records, and can be taken as providing a definite answer.

## Appendix 5 (from page 74)

WHEN THE survivors of the *Grasshopper* and *Dragonfly* decided that Padang was the only possible escape route, Petty Officer George White and two other men opted to remain on the island of Sinkep in the hope of eventually being able to make their way southward to Java and beyond.

Although Judy went with the others through the jungle, how these three men escaped from the Japanese is so extraordinary that it has a place in this book. The men took on the open sea, just as that great seaman Bligh did many years before. This is Petty Officer White's account of :

### The Incredible Voyage

I felt very sad at saying goodbye to my friends and shipmates—and to Judy. She seemed to understand all that was going on and licked my hand before I turned away. I was firmly convinced that there was no longer safety in numbers and that the Japanese would eventually round up all refugees and escapees. I also decided I was not going to be around when they did so.

With the others gone on their way I and my two companions—Engineer Lieutenant "Tommo" Thompson, RNVR, and Able Seaman "Tancy" Lee of the *Grasshopper*—re-attached ourselves to the Dutch Administrator at Dabo who seemed to be the only one in a position to help us.

He was a wonderful man. A constant stream of refugees and escapers were passing through his hands on the escape routes to Sumatra and Java. He gave them food, advice, and his blessing, knowing full well what his reward would be if—or when—the Japs caught up with him.

He was, however, unable to further our escape bid, and believed that we should have gone with our friends when they left Sinkep for Sumatra.

We tried, unsuccessfully, to obtain a boat in which to sail south. Desperate as we were, we could not bring ourselves to steal one from the kindly people who had already done so much for us.

I had reasoned that the Japs, after over-running Malaya, would soon turn their attention to Sumatra, and, in fact, they were even then dropping paratroops at Palembang and running troop transport convoys to the north and centre of the island.

On Sinkep, a relatively small island, we were safe for the time being, and we hoped we would be able to thumb a lift southward or, failing that, join up with any escapers who could afford to buy a boat.

Everyone else had similar ideas, of course.

Three Australians approached me with an invitation to join them in their plan, in which they proposed, after dark, to sail to an island off which a Japanese Gunboat was anchored. They would climb aboard, take over, then steam to Australia. As there were only three of them they thought they could do with more help!

Australians have always appeared to me to be larger than life and capable of almost anything, but their plan frightened the life out of me. They couldn't understand my blunt refusal, and went off to tackle it on their own.

Dutchy—as we called our friend the Dutch administrator—then decided that it would be best for all concerned if we left Sinkep, and arranged for us to go to a friend of his on the nearby and very much smaller island of Selajar. We had collected two other wanderers, both Army men, who had decided to throw in their lot with ours. There was only time for "Shake hands, join the club," then we were off, just the five of us. We were :

Lieutenant "Tommo" Thompson, RNVR, of Australia and Britain;

RSM "Sarge" Lamport, Army and Brighton;

Able Seaman "Tancy" Lee, *Grasshopper* and Liverpool;

"Gunner" Fixter, Army and Grimsby;

Myself—Petty Officer Coxswain George White, *Grasshopper* and Portsmouth. My nickname was Skipper.

The two boatmen who had been detailed to escort us to our new hide-out landed us at a small jetty at the little village of Penuba on Selajar, a picturesque village of thatched huts huddled against a background of palm trees and brush.

The islanders, who looked like Malays, wore sarongs and both men and women were bare-breasted. They were pleasant to look upon, but all our thoughts were directed towards our chance of survival.

Our new host was a Chinese gentleman—and I mean gentleman. His fifteen-year-old son, who had been to Grammar School in Singapore, acted as our interpreter when we told him who we were, where we had come from, and what we hoped to do. I can never understand why no one laughed outright at our declared determination to go home. At that stage it was only a matter of time, and not much time at that, before the Japanese occupied the whole of Sumatra, Java, and all the smaller islands in that part of the world. As far as we knew, they could in fact, already have done so.

Introductions over, we were shown to a hut which was to be our home for as long as we wished to stay, or for as long as the Japs would let us. We were well fed and taken care of. There was little that we could do in return for their kindness but as we could hardly sit on our behinds all day and wait for meal-time hand-outs, we did what we could.

We helped with the wood-cutting and refuse collecting, and, as with all sailors in any part of the world, we were soon on very friendly terms with the children and joining in some of their games. Not *all* games—we didn't like the one where you had to find, then pick up, live scorpions.

On our second night at Penuba we were awakened by a terrific hullabaloo. We gathered that natives from another island were raiding Penuba so we, too, rushed down to the beach to shout and yell with the others. Perhaps the raiders thought we were soldiers or police, or even Japanese. Whatever the reason, the raid suddenly petered out and we were being profusely thanked for our timely intervention.

Next morning our host's son, whom we called Jimmy, thanked us on behalf of his father who invited us to dinner that evening. We gratefully accepted and spent the rest of the day washing our clothes and making ourselves as presentable as possible.

When, that evening, we met our host—who was soon to be our friend and counsellor—he looked exactly as I had always imagined a mandarin would look. He wore long flowing robes of gold, silver, red and green. On his head was a small pill-box hat from beneath which hung a long pigtail. A white drooping moustache and goatee beard added to the overall impression of grandeur and wisdom.

After bidding us welcome to his house he ushered us into another room in which a long low table was groaning under its load of choice foods and fruit. His two lovely daughters waited on us; Jimmy acted as interpreter.

Jimmy laughed loudly at my look of consternation as I looked down at my first plateful. A huge eye, cold and baleful, was staring at me from the top of the heaped food. Thompson, who had lived in that part of the world before the war, dug me in the ribs with his elbow and hissed,

"Eat it! It's only a fish eye, usually given to the guest of honour."

We had been provided with beautiful china spoons in place of chopsticks and as though I ate fish eyes at every meal, I calmly scooped up the now accusing eye, gulped, smiled weakly at my host, then tucked into the food. We were off to a good start, anyhow.

It was a wonderful meal. Afterwards, over drinks and cigarettes, we talked well into the night. We told our host about our ships, of how we had fared since leaving Singapore, and of our hopes for the future. He said very little in reply; just nodded his head from time to time, and I had the impression that he was weighing us up.

If he was, then the scales must have tipped in our favour, for the following morning Jimmy came to us with a message from his father. Would we like a boat?

A boat—a big boat!

We rushed Jimmy to the small creek in which the boat lay partly hidden by the overgrown undergrowth. It had, quite obviously, not been used for a very long time. There was a large hole in the port bow. There was an engine in it, but it appeared to be solid with rust.

Jimmy's enthusiasm, however, backed up by the production of hammer, nails, wood, sacking, oil and spanners from his father's house, soon aroused our own enthusiasm again, and we set to work with a will. I put Lee and Thompson on the engine, Fixter on general clean-up, while Lamport assisted me in putting a tingle (nautical name for a patch) over the hole. Lamport and I were up to our hips in mud but we managed to do a fairly good job.

That evening and well into the night, we made our first definite plans for a getaway. Jimmy—God bless him—tore a map of the Indian Ocean from his school atlas, which he gave to me along with a notebook and pencil. I decided that the best route home would be northward between Malay and Sumatra, then westward for India. I would aim for Madras rather than Colombo as this would allow plenty of latitude both above and below my target.

As I enthusiastically pointed out to my admiring audience, it was only a distance of 2,680 miles, so we should do it comfortably in under three weeks—and this with no sails, no oars, and, at the moment, no engine!

The next day was one of mixed emotions. Jimmy told us that the Japs were visiting all the local islands to make it clear that they had taken over. During the morning, a boat chugged into the bay bringing the expected visitors —a Japanese Officer with six soldiers. They informed us that they were putting all islands under Japanese control, asked a few questions, then, after telling us to stay where we were for the time being, they went on to the next island.

It was now or never.

By noon our boat was afloat. Early in the afternoon we were grinning at each other as Thompson, with a dramatic flourish, started the engine. It was a Ruston & Hornsby Two-stroke engine and it seemed to me to make enough noise to be heard in Singapore.

All we needed now was time, and the blessings of the Almighty—and don't think I didn't ask for it.

We also needed much more fuel for the engine, so we made the short trip to Sinkep to see Dutchy. That wonderful man gave us four drums of diesel oil, some rice, a cigar each, and a bottle of Bols Gin. We then said goodbye to him and his people, and headed back to Penuba.

That evening we made our final preparations. The boat seemed sound enough. It was about the size of a Naval Whaler—25 feet by 8 feet, with a freeboard of 3 feet. We had four drums of fuel, a can of oil, rice, dried bananas, and fresh water. We had a rifle and five rounds, a pistol with no rounds, Thompson's watch, and one blanket. We were given large straw hats for protection against sun and rain, and armfuls of big leaves with which to cover the oil drums and provisions.

Until we had cleared Sumatra and Malaya we would travel by night and hole up during the day, so, deciding to make an immediate start, we manned the boat.

At the third attempt, the engine started. A last handshake from Jimmy, who was nearly in tears, and we were off. The first entry in my notebook read :

"April 11, 1942. Weather good. Left Penuba. God be with us."

The notebook was my log, in which I entered anything that happened, when it happened—and I'm afraid it was to happen very soon.

After a very cold but uneventful night, we were going along at about seven knots. Lamport was holding a bowl of rice, well soaked during the night, over the engine to get it warm. Thompson was rubbing his cold limbs and humming a hymn—it was Sunday morning.

Lee suddenly raised his head and said, "Listen!"

My heart sank as I heard the sound of a plane coming up fast astern. We kept our heads down as the plane swept low over us, turned, then roared back for a second look. It was a Jap plane, sure enough. I watched it rise into the clear sky and disappear in the direction of Singapore. Would he report having seen our boat? Would they send another plane?—or would we soon meet a searching Gunboat or destroyer?

We were all a bit worried. Thompson's fingers were so tightly crossed that his hands were white.

Worries?—It never rains but it pours. Thompson pointed out that we were leaking rather badly at the bows, and that we would soon have to do something about it.

Lee was breaking out in a mass of big boils which needed some sort of attention.

Gunner Fixter then staggered us by saying that he had made up his mind to leave us, and would I please put him ashore? Just like that! Gunner Fixter was quite sure that our trip was already doomed to failure. Furthermore he did not like the sea, and would not face the prospect of trying to cross the Indian Ocean in such a small boat. We tried to reason with him, but he was quite determined to leave us.

I had already decided to beach our boat for repairs, so we closed in nearer to the coast of Sumatra. Gunner Fixter was hoping that he might be able to rejoin our main party who were then, we thought, in Sumatra heading for Padang. We had no way of knowing that they were even then prisoners of the Japanese.

The coast looked dark and unfriendly in the early morning light but the sun was coming up, it was already getting warm, and all eyes were kept skinned for an opening in the coastline. When we eventually saw one, I turned the boat into the small creek and ran her ashore. We then piled out and hauled the boat far enough out of the water to enable us to repair the bows.

Gunner Fixter prepared to leave us. We argued, pleaded, swore—all in vain. He didn't want us to leave him, but didn't want to go on with us.

He was in tears; so was I. It's a terrible thing to see a man cry, but none of us were very strong at that time— and I think we all had a feeling that a wrong decision could easily mean death, his or ours.

We gave him all the money that we had between us, one fifth of the food, the rifle and five rounds, and made him drink his fill of the water, as we had nothing in which he could carry water. He shook hands all round, then made off into the swampy jungle.

We were all very upset, but there was work to be done so we got cracking.

We soon completed the repairs. Lee then wanted us to doctor his boils, but I felt uneasy at the thought of Sumatra being over-run by the Japs, so we pushed the boat astern until she refloated, started the engine, then chugged out into the deeper water of the Straits.

Although tempted to keep going, day and night, I agreed that it would be pushing our luck, so we crept under the overhanging growth of one of the many small islands to rest up for the day.

We operated on some of Lee's boils as best we could, then had our frugal breakfast. Bad planning. We should have reversed the procedure.

That night—our fourth—we realised how right we were not to have travelled by day. We started off badly. As Thompson started the engine he let loose a stream of words that would have turned a Chief Stoker green with envy. A piece of the engine's control gear had broken off, and it would now have to run continuously—night and day. No more stopping and starting.

I wasn't too despondent about this as we were making good progress up the Malacca Strait. As soon as we cleared Sumatra we could turn into the open sea and belt for India and safety.

It suddenly decided to rain. The average rainfall around there is about sixty inches. I reckon we had fifty-nine of them, and we had to bail like mad. We topped up our water tank by guiding the water down the outspread blanket, then used the blanket in an attempt to shield the boat.

Lee suddenly rasped : "Quiet !"

We froze. Straining our eyes, we could see two ships lying at anchor. Now unable to stop the engine, I veered off to give them as wide a berth as possible. Please God, if you are a fifth member of our crew, we need your help now.

We had almost run into two Japanese Transport vessels. I could make out the Japanese ensign at the stern of the nearest, but there was no sign of life on board.

Expecting to hear a yell, or a shot, we chugged past. The engine seemed to be noisier than ever. The rain still belted down. Nothing happened. We left them behind us and headed for the Indian Ocean.

We ploughed on through the night and at dawn I turned in towards the coast of Sumatra, but just where I didn't know. There would be no "TURN LEFT" sign, and I did not want to go too far north and so waste our precious fuel.

It was then that the Jap bomber arrived. He came down low and circled us. I thanked God for our big straw hats as my bald head was not sunburnt and it would have shown like a full moon. I turned to port as though to show the pilot that we were going ashore, and gave what I hoped was a laconic wave. The bomber made off.

All these excitements were not good for us. We were not strong enough for such shocks. My own heart-beats were louder than the engine's.

A school of dolphins joined up with us as though to encourage us. Some say they are a good omen. I hoped they were. We had been very lucky so far, although I secretly believed that my prayers had been answered. Like most naval men, I believe in the power of prayer. Not for things like double pay on pay-days, but for really important things—especially for others. You may not get the answer you expected, but it will be the right one in the end.

During the next day we saw the Sumatra coast disappear completely, so I altered course to North West.

We were all very cheerful in the knowledge that we were at last in the Indian Ocean with our bows pointed directly (I hoped!) at Madras.

Lee's boils must have been very painful, but he didn't complain. A few choice words when we doctored him, but that's all. He and Thompson kept the engine running like a bomb. Lamport and I took turns at steering. We steered by the stars at night, and by the sun during the day. When neither was visible I kept the sea running in the same relative direction, and hoped for the best.

As much for something to do as anything, I proposed

F

that we should try a simple experiment to calculate our
speed through the water. I put Lamport in the bows, with
myself at the stern. Lamport then dropped a coconut shell
into the sea; I yelled as it passed the stern. Thompson,
watch in hand, then gave us the time that it had taken to
travel along our twenty-five feet length.

The first reading gave us a time of three seconds and a
calculated speed of almost five knots. The second attempt,
with the now-empty gin bottle, produced a time of one-
and-a-half seconds—a speed of nearly ten knots.

When I explained that the boat was of insufficient
length to give accuracy, Lee suggested that I should be
towed well astern so that I could shout as the next marker
passed us. I declared the experiment at an end.

Sunday morning again, we had been going for more than
a week, and the worst was behind us—I hoped. Although
not very strong, we were all in good spirits, so I decided to
carry out the Navy's usual Sunday morning routine—
Hands to Prayers.

I said prayers for us all, and gave thanks, then we sang
a couple of hymns with great gusto. I could easily imagine
the scene in any Naval Barracks church on that Sunday
morning. They always sang Jack's favourite—"For those
in peril on the sea". That meant us! We would have
boosted the Padre's takings to an all-time record if we
could only have been in his congregation just then.

The sea was a bit rough, but not too bad. I was surprised that no one was seasick. Not enough food in us, perhaps. Although we had little food we still had to obey the
calls of nature.

It was pretty grim having to hang on to your chum as
he squatted over the stern, but it had to be done.

I always had the fear that a shark or something would
make a sudden snatch at what it thought was dangling
bait!

I was tempted at that time, to head for the Nicobar group
of islands, which I then thought to be north of me, but I

didn't know how many islands were now in Japanese hands.

The next day brought changes. The sky became over-cast, and a good breeze blew from astern. We should be safe from aircraft anyhow.

Thompson was obviously a sick man. He thought it was malaria, which he had had before. We made him lie down, and gave him everything we had to keep him warm. Lamport tended to his needs—water, toilet, and so on. Lee looked after the engine. All we could do then was to steer a steady course and hope for the best. We were doing quite well up to then except for Thompson's malaria. Another five days should see us in India.

This was hardly a "round the harbour for five bob" trip, but we were, if not in good health, in very good spirits.

We talked a lot—about this and that, and generally put the world to rights. Lamport had a very dry humour. I remember that Lee and I were gnawing the hardy perennial of mess-deck arguments—which was of most importance, fire or water. We finally appealed to Lamport to give his opinion.

He immediately decided that water was of the greatest importance. When asked to give his reasons he replied : "Well, if it wasn't for water we'd have to push this damned boat all the way."

That was the thirteenth day, a day that could well have been our unluckiest.

What appeared to be a small island suddenly emerged just off our port bow. We all saw it, then it disappeared just as suddenly, only to re-appear, a few minutes later, on the starboard side. That time, however, it remained wholly below the surface—a huge indistinguishable mass keeping pace with the boat.

We couldn't make out just what it was—a whale?—a huge ray?—an octopus? It remained with us for about fifteen minutes then again disappeared—for good.

For a long time afterwards I half expected a huge mouth to swallow us up, or a long tentacle to snake into the boat, but nothing happened, and eventually I stopped worrying about it.

On the fourteenth day, Lee was worrying about the fuel, which was then very low in our last drum.

I was worrying, too, supposing I had gone in a circle and was now heading for Sumatra! or suppose I had missed India altogether!

Thompson by now was very sick. Lamport didn't look too good, either. As much for their sakes as for my own, I prayed like mad while I boldly foretold that we would sight land within the next twenty-four hours. I didn't say *what* land, but it cheered everyone up.

We did, too! The next day, in the afternoon, there it was! Lovely, real land. We were hugging each other laughing—or crying—or both. I heard Lee saying : "Keep going, little engine. You've done a wonderful job for us. I'd kiss you if you weren't so hot."

It kept going. The land came nearer and nearer. We could hear surf; see people. We yelled like mad, then the water was very rough and the boat was turning over. We grabbed Thompson and struggled for the beach. Helping hands grasped us—and we were ashore. We had made it!

On the beach we were surrounded by natives all chattering at once until one, more authoritative than the others, questioned us in fairly good English. Satisfied that we were not the enemy, he sent a runner to the nearby Pulicat Lighthouse.

Soon afterwards an Englishman arrived in a car and carried us off to his house. A few questions, then we were allowed to bathe and eat before being shown beds where we slept for the night. Our host had only to contact the Naval Authorities at Madras—twenty-three miles away —and the journey was over. We had done it—2,680 miles we had travelled. It had taken us nearly seventeen days and yet we had only missed the target by twenty-three miles.

Our decision to leave the main group and go it alone was vindicated. For us the war was over. For the ones who went the other way, it was just beginning.

# EXTRACT FROM THE PORTSMOUTH "EVENING NEWS"

## July 27, 1942

FEELING VERY humble, I sat in the front room of Number 120, Knox Road, Portsmouth, and listened to Petty Officer George Leonard White telling me of how he and three companions, in an open boat, voyaged for 2,600 miles across the Indian Ocean.

"I plotted my course on here," he said, producing a map torn from an old Dutch school atlas. "You can see that I was trying to reach Madras, but we landed twenty-three miles north of that city."

They were his words to describe a feat of navigation which was carried out in a leaky boat, with a schoolboy's atlas, a two-foot rule, and a pencil. The story of the voyage, written in pencil in a notebook log, is a story of steadfastness and determination which can have few equals in the whole history of the Royal Navy.

Extract from : Royal Artillery Records
                Foots Cray, Sidcup, Kent.


*RSM Lamport*
1422106 WO11 Lamport GB RA 1st India Coast Battery
Arrived in India from Singapore April 1942
Died in No 5 Base Camp, India, of paratyphoid.


*Gunner Fixter*
922763 Gunner Fixter FJ RA (HQ 18th Division)
Taken prisoner by Japanese early 1942 in Sumatra
Died July 1943 in Thailand (POW in Japanese hands)
of beri-beri.


*Lieut (E) RNR Thompson*
Mentioned in despatches, November 24th, 1942
Demobilised as Lieut. Commander 1946
Died April 1st, 1958.


*AB Lee*
No trace after the war.